TO

FROM

DATE

Dear Single Mom, YOU'RE DOING GREAT!

Devotions of God's Love amid the Chaos

DaySpring
LIVE YOUR FAITH

Dear Single Mom, You're Doing Great! Devotions of God's Love amid the Chaos

First Edition, February 2025

Published by:

DaySpring

21154 Highway 16 East
Siloam Springs, AR 72761
dayspring.com

Written by: Christy Phillippe
Cover Design by: Jenna Wilusz

Printed in China
Prime: U2775
ISBN: 979-8-88602-876-8

CONTENTS

Introduction 9
What Matters Most 10
Mommy Tasks 12
You're Not Alone 14
Pool Inflatables, One; Single Mom, Zero 16
Provided For 18
Beyond the Tears 20
Fear Is Not Your Friend 22
Celebrate the Little Victories 24
Warning! Brain Overload! 26
Keep on Dreaming 28
Necessary Rest 32
A Brighter Tomorrow 34
Getting Along 36
"It's Complicated" 38
Living a Life of Trust 40
A Listening Ear 42
Coming Home 44
Renewed Strength 46
Learning to Thrive 48
A Lighter Burden 50
You've Got This! 54

Danger and Opportunity 56
The Never-Ending To-Do List 58
Eager Anticipation 60
Choosing Grace 62
Letting Go of the Mess 64
Renewed Hope 66
The Beauty of Unexpected Moments 68
Make Time to Laugh! 70
The Safety Net of Community 72
Mom Guilt 76
"Not Fair!" 78
The Widow's Reward 80
Lost in the Desert 82
A Daughter of God 84
The Web of Guilt 86
Rest for the Weary, Peace for the Worn Out 88
Asking for Help 90
Remembering Your Purpose 92
Let Go of the Hustle 94
He Knows Your Needs 98
Who Are You? 100
Jesus' Rest 102
"Come Here!" 104
Beauty in Unexpected Places 106
An Attitude of Gratitude 108

Let. It. Go.. 110
Yes, You Can. 112
Sleeping through the Storm 114
Sharing the Real You 116
If You Need to Recharge, Unplug! 120
Reach Out to Him 122
Pleasing God, Not People 124
Don't Be a Worrywart! 126
The Maker of the Trees 128
A Season for All Things 130
The Running of My World 132
This Very Moment. 134
Honest Forgiveness. 136
Money Matters 138
Listen to Your Body. 142
"O Normal Day!" 144
Clothed with Compassion 146
The Ultimate Friend 148
Run the Race 150
Betrayed with a Kiss 152
Everything. Yes, *Every*thing! 154
Rest for Your Soul 156
Enjoy the Little Things 158
Dream Big 160
New Life Ahead 164

What No Thief Can Steal 166
Never Alone 168
The Journey of Forgiveness 170
Happily Ever After 172
He's Ready to Listen 174
Think on These Things 176
A Beautiful Work of His Hand 178
Restoration Awaits 180
Be an Example 182
Tune in to the Kids 186
Guard Your Heart! 188
A Bright Future 190
A New Perspective 192
Love Your Enemies 194
Someone Who Understands 196
True Love 198
What's Your Worth? 200
Take Care of Yourself! 202
Writing Your Story 204

INTRODUCTION

Dear Friend,

If you have picked up this book, it's likely that you, like me, are a single mom. My story may be like yours, or it could be completely different. I was thrust unwillingly into single motherhood when I filed for divorce in 2016, after circumstances that shocked my senses and threw my life—and the lives of my two children—into absolute chaos. The kids were little—Tucker was just seven, and Gracie was four years old. We found ourselves escorted in the middle of the night by the police to a secure domestic violence shelter—an unfamiliar setting for us, to be sure! The events of the months, and years, that followed were just as unfamiliar: court battles, leaving the only home my kids had ever known, financial scarcity where once there had been security. But through it all, God was so faithful. We have never gone hungry, never missed a meal, and neither of my children have ever had to go without something they really wanted. Today, we are *somewhat* on the other side. Challenges still face us every day, but now that the years have passed (Tucker is in now high school, and Gracie is going into seventh grade!), those super-dark days are firmly in the rearview mirror. We are no longer just *surviving*, but I can honestly say that we are *thriving*; our menagerie of pets, busy schedules, and a house constantly filled with love and laughter prove just that!

Wherever you are on your journey of single motherhood, whether you are divorced, widowed, or were never married at all, please know that God loves you, and He is right there, waiting to help. I'm living proof of that!

Blessings,

Christy

WHAT MATTERS MOST

And my God will liberally supply
(fill until full) your every need according to
His riches in glory in Christ Jesus.
PHILIPPIANS 4:19 AMP

"Moooommmmmm!" my youngest pleaded as I tried to negotiate the grocery cart past the toy aisle before she noticed the newest "thing" to hit the shelves. It might have been a new L.O.L. doll, Hatchimal, or LEGO set. But who was I kidding? She'd likely already seen it, either at a friend's house or on one of those (horribly unnecessary) "toy un-packaging" channels on YouTube.

The thing was, not that long ago, I could have afforded to buy her a new toy—even a small one as a reward for her good behavior in the store. But that was when we were a two-income, still-married household. Now it was just me, and some days it was a challenge just getting food on the table and paying the bills on time. The guilt nagged at me.

"Maybe next time, honey," I said as we headed to the checkout lanes. My daughter sighed, but then she smiled at me. "Okay, Mom. I get it," she said, and I reminded myself that kids are resilient, after all.

In a world that often equates worth with material possessions, it's easy to succumb to the pressure of providing the latest gadgets or designer clothes for our children. But as a single mom, the desire to give our kids the world can sometimes be overshadowed by the weight of our financial limitations.

Dear Mama, it's time to take a step back and take a deep breath. More than anything else, your kids need YOU—a healthy, happy mom who loves them, who spends time with them, and who points them toward their loving heavenly Father who is always there for them.

Laughter, hugs, bedtime stories—the value you offer your children is worth far more than the price tag of any new whatever-that-new-hot-thing-is. As you release the burden of comparison and embrace the uniqueness of your own parenting journey, don't forget: your kids aren't defined by the possessions they own, but by the love they receive and the values you are teaching. So keep up the good work, Mama! Your kiddos are worth it.

Dear Lord,

sometimes I feel so guilty about what I can and can't provide for my kids. Help me to remember that You are more than enough for us and that You will always give us just what we need. As I continue to teach my children about You and Your ways, I pray that You will bless our family, each of my kids, right where we are. Thank You for Your love and grace!

Amen.

MOMMY TASKS

Trust in the Lord with all your heart;
do not depend on your own understanding.
Seek His will in all you do,
and He will show you which path to take!

PROVERBS 3:5–6

When the kids are little, it seems the mommy tasks will never end. Diaper changes, late-night feedings, tummy time, and playdates fill the days. As they get a little older, soon you find yourself making homemade Play-Doh for the kindergarten class or getting talked into being your son's fourth-grade homeroom parent. When "Mommy" transforms into "Mom," you think you might have it easier, but then there are sports tryouts, band practices, Girl Scout cookie sales, and driver's education until you are thinking about college applications.

Every stage of your child's development is precious, from babyhood to the teenage years and beyond. Watching your kiddos grow and blossom into the people they will become is one of the most amazing experiences life has to offer. But sometimes, Mama, it can seem daunting as you find yourself juggling . . . All. The. Things.

Let's face it. It's even more daunting doing it as a single mom. Remembering absolutely everything—from when library books are due to when permission slips need to be turned in—can seem almost impossible some days. But you know what? God picked you—yes, you—to be the mama of these particular kiddos, and He knew you could handle it! He knew what your circumstances would be, and He picked you just for them. You can do it, Mama. Take a deep breath, and realize that He is right by your side, today and on all the days from here on.

Lord,

sometimes all the things I have
to remember and keep track of overwhelm me.
Thank You for the reminder that I am not alone.
You are always with me.

Amen.

YOU'RE NOT ALONE

"Peace I leave with you;
My peace I give you.
I do not give to you as the world gives.
Do not let your hearts be troubled
and do not be afraid."

JOHN 14:27 NIV

I heard the cough from across the room. As the mom of a kid with asthma, I knew what that sound meant. The sneezing he'd been experiencing for a few days now was moving into his lungs. Many times he would be just fine after a few breathing treatments of albuterol from the nebulizer. But occasionally it got bad, a simple cold quickly turning into an ER visit, once with his lips turned blue from lack of oxygen. My mama's heart twisted in fear.

It's really inevitable. As a mom, we know these times of worry and fear will come, when we aren't sure if our little ones are going to be okay. And it can become even scarier when we feel like we are facing those times alone—without a husband or a partner to help us stay calm in the middle of the storm.

The good news is, we have Someone with us who is pretty well-known for calming actual, *literal* storms. Jesus is the Prince of Peace, and when you find yourself facing an overwhelming situation, one in which you don't know what to do or how things will turn out, you can *always* turn to Him. He's never asleep, not listening, not waiting to answer you when you need Him. "Don't be afraid," He says to you today. He's got the situation in hand, even if you feel you don't. And He will work it out.

Lord,

at times fear grips my heart, and I don't know what to do or where to turn. Thank You for always being there for me, for never leaving my side. I lay all of my worries and fears at Your feet today, trusting that You are holding me in Your loving hands.

Amen.

POOL INFLATABLES, ONE; SINGLE MOM, ZERO

A cheerful heart is good medicine,
but a crushed spirit dries up the bones.
PROVERBS 17:22 NIV

We were on our way to the pool, but we no longer had my husband's truck to load all our supplies. My kids still had their hearts set on taking the giant inflatable pizza slice and flamingo along. Rather than deflating them and trying to inflate them again at the community pool, it seemed easier to just strap them to the top of the car. *How hard could it be?* I wondered. *Men use bungee cords all the time to strap things down. Why not pool inflatables?*

Minutes later, we were on the way. "Uh, Mom," I heard my daughter say from the back seat. Her window had been rolled down for the fresh air, but now her head was craned outside, staring up at the sky as we drove down the highway.

"Mom! I think you should pull over!" my son cried out

from the front passenger seat, his head now also out the window.

What had happened? Our pool inflatables were airborne. The bungee cords had only half-held, and the pink flamingo and giant slice of pepperoni pizza were flapping wildly above our car, like kites gone crazy. Other vehicles sounded their horns as we pulled over. Of course, we were thankful nobody had gotten hurt—and that our inflatables were safe! And together we laughed hysterically as we deflated them by the side of the road before heading on to the pool. *All in a day in the life of a single mama!* I thought, thankful to God for the times of laughter I could have with my kids. I knew that was a story we would talk about for years!

In the chaos of daily life, it's so important to find joy in the little things. Sometimes it's the crazy mistakes a mom can make—other times it could be a "Godwink," a moment that tells you He is still in control when you know you're not!

Lord,

thank You for moments of laughter with my kids.
And thank You for Your protection in my craziest of days!

Amen.

PROVIDED FOR

"Look at the birds, free and unfettered,
not tied down to a job description,
careless in the care of God.
And you count far more to Him than birds."

MATTHEW 6:26 THE MESSAGE

The electric bill sat there on the table in front of me, and my stomach twisted. That day, pulling three hundred dollars together might as well have been like needing a million. *What am I gonna do?* I wondered. *Lord, please provide.*

A few hours later, an email hit my inbox. A new project. The client offered to send a deposit immediately—three hundred dollars. I was astonished—but I shouldn't have been. Even without a husband to provide for me and my precious children, we had a heavenly Father who never let us down. Even in our leanest times, we have never not had what we needed.

Mama, just as the sun rises on another day—and you can count on that every day—you can count on your heavenly Father to provide for you. Even if you are facing uncertainty this day, He is not. He sees the end before the beginning, and He's already made a way for you—to meet that need, to calm that fear, to make a way.

Each day will bring its own set of challenges—we know that is true! But even more true is the promise that God is an ever-present help in time of need. Even in our most challenging times, He stands ready to help. All you need to do is ask.

Lord,

thank You for Your provision in every area of my life.
With Your help, I know there is nothing in
my life that I can't handle this day.

Amen.

BEYOND THE TEARS

Weeping may last through the night,
but joy comes with the morning.

PSALM 30:5

I never expected to be a single mom. I'd always valued the stability a two-parent household provided for kids, and I did my best to make the marriage work—until I couldn't. Still, I never wanted my children to experience the sting of a family breakup. So, when it happened, the divorce nearly broke me—and truthfully, it took years to learn to let go of the pain.

Today, your heart, too, may be heavy with a pain that feels almost unbearable. Tears flow freely, and the weight of loss and grief seems to suffocate you. It's in these moments, when the world feels like it's crumbling around you, that it's hard to see beyond the darkness.

The psalmist also understood the depths of emotional trauma. He faced the looming shadows of devastation in his own life; yet, even in the midst of his despair, he held on to a glimmer of hope. He understood that beyond the tears, beyond the heartache, there was a promise of joy. He trusted in the assurance that tomorrow held the possibility of healing and restoration.

In your pain, it's natural if your faith wavers a bit. Mine sure did, especially in the beginning. But even if the road ahead seems long and uncertain, you are not alone. God, the Source of all comfort, stands beside you, ready to offer solace in your darkest moments. He sees your tears, hears your cries, and holds you close in His embrace.

Take courage, Mama—your tears will not last forever! Surround yourself with those who love you, who will walk alongside you and offer a shoulder to lean on. Though the journey may be difficult, there is hope on the horizon!

Lord,

I know You see my tears on my darkest days.
Thank You for being near and for Your promise
that joy will come in the morning.

Amen.

FEAR IS NOT YOUR FRIEND

Give all your worries and cares to God, for He cares about you.

1 PETER 5:7

My friends and I stood in line at the movie theater to get our tickets. It was a rare night out for me—especially to see a "grown-up" move (i.e., something *not* animated or showing on Disney+).

"Ma'am, I'm sorry. Your card was declined."

Panic seized my heart. I knew there was plenty of money in my account—or was there? Had I missed something? Had something been stolen?

Although my friend paid for my ticket that night, I spent the entire movie worrying until I could get home later and check my bank balance. I nearly made myself sick, and I missed the whole movie. Turns out—my balance was fine. It must have been a glitch in the system. But all that worry? It was for nothing.

Dear single mama, the weight of worry can often feel like an ever-present companion. It may seem like a natural response, a way to prepare for the unexpected challenges life may throw your way. Yet, in reality, worry serves only to drain your energy, leaving you depleted and anxious over imagined scenarios that may never come to pass.

In the face of worry and anxiety, the words of Jesus' friend Peter offer a beacon of hope. He urges us to release our burdens, casting our cares on Jesus, who is our refuge and strength. Clinging to worry, he suggests, is a subtle indication of a lack of trust in God's provision and care. Yet God stands ready to shoulder our worries, offering us peace in exchange for our burdens.

God is not distant or indifferent to your struggles, Mama. He is intimately involved in every aspect of your life, including your role as a single mom. Entrusting your worries to Him does not mean ignoring your responsibilities or challenges. Rather, it is an act of faith, acknowledging that He alone has the power to bring balance and peace to your life.

Choose to surrender your worries today to Jesus. Each time anxiety threatens to overwhelm you, consciously release it into His capable hands, trusting in His faithfulness to guide you and sustain you through everything you face today.

Lord,

I don't do myself any favors when I worry.
Help me to cast all my cares onto You today.
I know You care for me.

Amen.

CELEBRATE THE LITTLE VICTORIES

This is the day the LORD has made.
We will rejoice and be glad in it.
PSALM 118:24

Bedtime has come, and the kids are finally asleep. How much is left on *your* to-do list? I know that for me, mine was never . . . ever . . . done!

At the close of each day, it's all too easy to be weighed down by a sense of defeat. The unchecked boxes on our to-do lists seem to mock us, reminding us of all the tasks left undone. We dwell on missed deadlines, forgotten obligations, and the nagging feeling that we have fallen short once again.

What if, Mama, instead of fixating on our shortcomings, we chose to celebrate our triumphs? What if we took a moment to acknowledge and appreciate all that we *did* accomplish this day, no matter how small or seemingly insignificant?

Maybe it was just a day where you kept the kids alive until bedtime. We've all been there! Did they eat? Are they clean? Do they still have a roof over their heads? Good job, Mama. Did you offer a word of encouragement to a friend or tackle a challenging task you've been putting off? Extra points!

While today might not have unfolded exactly as planned, God will not waste your efforts. Each victory, no matter how small, is a testament to your resilience and determination.

Remember: Tomorrow is a new day, ripe with fresh opportunities and challenges. For now, rest in the knowledge that God delights in your efforts, however imperfect they may seem. Your willingness to persevere, to love, and to serve brings glory to His name, even in the midst of life's messy imperfections. So celebrate your successes, Mama, however humble they may be! You are seen, valued, and cherished by the One who created you!

Lord,

thank You for helping me throughout this day.
I choose to focus on the victories You and I have won
more than the challenges that weren't resolved,
and I look forward to a new day tomorrow!

Amen.

WARNING!
BRAIN OVERLOAD!

Instead of worrying, pray. Let petitions
and praises shape your worries into prayers,
letting God know your concerns.
Before you know it, a sense of God's wholeness,
everything coming together for good,
will come and settle you down.
It's wonderful what happens when Christ
displaces worry at the center of your life.

PHILIPPIANS 4:6–7 THE MESSAGE

In the whirlwind of daily life, do you ever feel like your mind is on overload? As a woman—and a single mom—the demands on your memory can often feel overwhelming. Each day, your brain becomes a repository for countless details, dates, and to-dos, tirelessly sorting out grocery lists, household chores, school and work projects, and more.

In our hurry-it-up society, our senses are bombarded with a constant stream of distractions. From the endless array of TV channels that take forever to scroll through so that you're too tired to watch once you've picked a program, to the omnipresence of social media, it's all too easy to succumb to the cacophony of noise vying for our attention. Without even realizing it, we willingly expose our minds to these external influences, allowing them to infiltrate our thoughts and shape our perceptions.

In the midst of this chaos, God calls us to care for our minds with intentionality and purpose. What are some good things you can think about today? (Hint: read Philippians 4:8 for some suggestions.)

If the constant buzz of activity threatens to overwhelm your mind, it may be time to pause and recalibrate. Turn off the television for a while, even if you use it for background noise or to entertain the kids while you get chores done. Silence your phone notifications for an hour if you can. Shut the bathroom door for five minutes and take a breather. Creating spaces of quiet in your day allows your mind to unwind and recharge, allowing you the clarity, insight, and renewed strength you need to get through the rest of the day.

God,

I need a little peace and quiet today. Help me to carve out time with You to recharge my spirit and rest.

Amen.

KEEP ON DREAMING

Just as you cannot understand the path of the wind
or the mystery of a tiny baby growing in its mother's womb,
so you cannot understand the activity of God,
who does all things.

ECCLESIASTES 11:5

When you were a little girl, did your heart overflow with dreams and aspirations for the future? Did you envision yourself as a princess, a mermaid, a ballerina? How about when you got older—did you want to become a teacher, a lawyer, a doctor, even a cupcake decorator? Regardless of what you hoped to be, you likely dared to imagine a life filled with adventure and fulfillment.

Yet, as we journey through the complexities of adulthood—navigating high school, maybe college, along with grown-up relationships, engagements, and marriage—our lives often unfold in unexpected ways. Some of our childhood dreams may come to fruition, but many remain elusive, lost amid the twists and turns of life's journey.

Does your reality look vastly different from the dreams you once held dear? Perhaps you longed for the joy of marriage or the blessing of more children, yet you find yourself still waiting for those desires to be fulfilled. Maybe the career you pursued with passion and dedication fails to bring the fulfillment you had hoped for, or your financial security falls short of your expectations. In the face of shattered hopes and dashed dreams, life can feel unbearably challenging.

If you find yourself grappling with disappointment and disillusionment, take heart in the knowledge that you are not alone. The Lord sees your struggles, understands your frustrations, and longs to offer you comfort and hope in the midst of your pain. He invites you to pour out your heart to Him, to confide in Him your deepest fears, disappointments, and desires. He is not only a God who listens, but a God who cares deeply about every facet of your life.

Dear Mama, in the midst of all you are doing today, trust that God can take the broken pieces of your dreams and weave them into the beautiful tapestry of His divine plan. Though the road may be full of uncertainty and hardship, have faith that He is working all things together for your good and His glory. Your disappointments need not be the end of the story; they can become the fertile ground in which God's purpose for your life takes root and flourishes.

Lord,

I may not understand right now all the ways You are working in my life, but I choose to put my trust in You.

Amen.

CHILDREN ARE A GIFT FROM THE LORD;

THEY ARE
A REWARD
FROM HIM.

Psalm 127:3

NECESSARY REST

It is useless for you to work so hard
from early morning until late at night,
anxiously working for food to eat;
for God gives rest to His loved ones.
—PSALM 127:2

In a world that glorifies productivity and celebrates the hustle, the pressure to constantly be on the go can feel suffocating. From dawn till dusk, the life of a single mama is often consumed by a relentless pursuit of tasks and accomplishments. Long workdays bleed into evenings, and weekends blur into an extension of the workweek. Even in our moments of rest, the omnipresent glow of our electronic devices beckons, demanding our attention and tethering us to the never-ending cycle of busyness.

In the middle of this cultural obsession with productivity, there exists a sacred invitation—a beckoning to rest. It's a call to pause, to step away from the frenetic pace of life, and to find solace in the quiet rhythms of Sabbath rest.

Rest is not merely a luxury; it is a necessity—an essential component of our physical, emotional, and spiritual well-being. And yet, in a society that prizes productivity above all else, rest is often dismissed as frivolous or unnecessary. But the truth remains: rest is vital for our health and wholeness, and it is a gift bestowed upon us by a loving and gracious God.

In the midst of our relentless pursuit of productivity, we must dare to defy the status quo. We must learn to rest without hesitation, without guilt, and without apology. We must carve out moments of respite amid the chaos of our daily lives, prioritizing time with our families, with our Creator, and in communion with the natural world He has so beautifully crafted.

It's natural to feel the weight of expectation bearing down upon us—the fear that the world will come crashing down if we dare to step away from our endless to-do lists. But we must push back against these lies, recognizing that our worth is not contingent upon our productivity. We are beloved daughters of God Himself, and He invites us to lay down our burdens and find rest in Him.

I need to rest, Lord,

but I have so much to do. Help me remember that productivity isn't the most important thing in life, and that it's okay to step back and relax for a while. In fact, it's what You ask me to do.

Amen.

A BRIGHTER TOMORROW

"Then [with a deep longing] you will seek Me and require Me [as a vital necessity] and [you will] find Me when you search for Me with all your heart."

JEREMIAH 29:13 AMP

I grew up in a happy, two-parent home, and that's what I expected my kids to have, too. The idea that they could be missing out on such an idyllic childhood weighed heavily on me for a long time after the divorce was final.

It's part of our human nature, isn't it? That innate inclination to seek something better, to aspire toward a brighter tomorrow. This pursuit is especially poignant within the realm of motherhood, where the fervent desire to provide a better life for our children burns brightly within our hearts. It's a profound reflection of our optimism and perseverance, manifesting in our relentless pursuit of solutions amid life's inevitable trials and tribulations.

The theme of seeking something better resonates deeply throughout the Bible. Even in the words spoken to the prophet Jeremiah, God extended an invitation to His people, promising that if they sought Him with unwavering devotion, they would surely find Him. Jesus also reiterated this divine invitation to His disciples, reassuring them with these words: "Ask and it will be given to you; seek and you will find; knock and the door will be opened to you" (Matthew 7:7 NIV). It was a tender acknowledgment of life's inherent challenges, coupled with a steadfast persistence to seek the solace and solutions found in a relationship with God.

Dear single mama, when you lift your voice to the Lord, it transcends mere words; it becomes a heartfelt plea, and God is not indifferent. He knows your hopes and dreams for your kids, and He loves them as much as you do! He is intimately present with both you and your children, and He will provide you all with everything you need.

Lord,

I know You have amazing plans, not only for me, but also for my children—and You never disappoint. Thank You for loving us just as we are and providing everything we could ever need.

Amen.

GETTING ALONG

Make every effort to live in peace with everyone and to be holy; without holiness no one will see the Lord.

HEBREWS 12:14 NIV

Relationships are so important to our lives, aren't they? Without them, life would be dull and boring. But they can be a mixed bag sometimes. Sometimes they are smooth sailing, and other times—well, they feel more like a stormy sea.

Whether it's our relationship with our ex-spouse or partner, our parents, colleagues, friends—or even our own kiddos, conflict seems to find its way into every nook and cranny of our lives at times. We are all a bit rough around the edges, aren't we? We all mess up, say things we regret, and sometimes unintentionally hurt the ones we care about the most.

So, here's a question for you, single mama: Is there someone in your life who just seems to stir up a whirlwind of emotions every time you cross paths? Does thinking about them make your stomach tie up in knots or keep you tossing and turning at night? If that's a yes, then it's time to bring that burden to the Lord.

Navigating the choppy waters of broken relationships

isn't easy. It's like trying to untangle a mess of cords behind your TV—frustrating, messy, and downright exhausting. But here's the good news: when you've got God on your side, things start to look a whole lot brighter.

So why not take a moment today to spend some time with the best Friend you could ever have? Your relationship status with Him doesn't need to be "it's complicated"! Pour out your heart and spill the tea on what's been weighing you down. Trust me, He's all ears, and He's got a knack for shining a light on the truth buried beneath all the drama. He can guide you through all the relational storms of your life with grace and love.

God,

help me to live in peace with those around me today—
especially those whom I find the most challenging.
Thank You for Your grace,
which is present in all my relationships.

Amen.

"IT'S COMPLICATED"

How long, Lord? Will You forget me forever?
How long will You hide Your face from me? . . .
But I trust in Your unfailing love;
my heart rejoices in Your salvation.
I will sing the Lord's praise,
for He has been good to me.

PSALM 13:1, 5–6 NIV

Let's face it: divorce can get ugly. Uglier than an ugly cry behind the bathroom door, am I right? And in the aftermath, trying to co-parent with an ex gets complicated—fast.

Maybe an ex-spouse isn't a problem in your life, but someone else is. In the tapestry that weaves the fabric of our lives, woven among the threads of joy and triumph are the knots of difficult relationships. At some point, we all grapple with the complexities of connections, whether it's with parents, ex-spouses, siblings, fellow church members, colleagues, friends, or even our own children. We are flawed beings, prone to saying and doing things that wound others, often hindered by the barriers of ego and past traumas, preventing authentic connection.

Do you find yourself entangled in a tumultuous relationship today? Does it weigh heavy on your heart, causing anxiety and sleepless nights? When thoughts of that person stir a knot in your stomach, it's time to turn to the Lord in earnest prayer. Invite Him into the depths of your turmoil, asking for His divine wisdom to illuminate the path forward.

Navigating the treacherous terrain of broken relationships can be an arduous journey, but when you walk hand in hand with the Lord, His presence becomes a beacon of hope in the middle of the challenges. Entrust Him with the weight of your burdens and ask Him to infuse your heart with His peace. He is faithful to guide you in all your relationships, and He delights in offering strength and wisdom in the midst of every challenge you face.

Some people, Lord, try my patience,
and it's hard to walk in peace with them.
Help me to hold my tongue when I need to,
walk in love when I should, and
show Your grace today and always,
even in my most tumultuous relationships.
Amen.

LIVING A LIFE OF TRUST

In God have I put my trust
and confident reliance;
I will not be afraid.
What can man do to me?
PSALM 56:11 AMP

My dad loved trees. And as I was growing up in Central Florida, there were plenty of trees around to climb—some of them with really tall branches, others with low-swinging vines with Spanish moss. Dad and I spent hours climbing trees together, with him always watching out to make sure I didn't fall or get hurt.

Did you ever try something "dangerous" as a kid? Maybe it was climbing a tree or learning to ride a bike without training wheels, or even learning how to swim in the deep end without floaties on your arms. The best way to overcome your fear in those situations was to trust that your parent or another loving adult would not let you fall or get hurt as you were learning to do these things. Kneepads, helmets, floaties, ropes, even a lifeguard nearby—they certainly helped ease the nerves!

Now, as a mom, you're on the flip side of that trust equation. You get to experience the same exercise in trust, but this time from the perspective of the one holding the reins. With your child's safety as your top priority, you navigate through the fears and uncertainties, always striving to keep them safe and secure.

The psalmist captured the essence of this trust beautifully. He spoke of the incredible power of trust, especially in the face of fear. And let's face it: life throws its fair share of curveballs our way. Jesus Himself warned us that life wouldn't always be smooth sailing (John 16:33). But here's the thing—it's in those very moments of fear and uncertainty that our trust in God shines the brightest.

God, I trust in You.

I know You care for both me and my children, and I choose to rest in Your loving arms today.

Amen.

A LISTENING EAR

"Anyone who belongs to God
listens gladly to the words of God."
JOHN 8:47

Picture this: Your home is alive with the warmth of friendship as you gather around the dinner table with loved ones. Amid the laughter and clinking of utensils, soft melodies fill the air, creating a cozy ambiance. And then, in the middle of the joyful chaos, you suddenly rise from your seat and rush out. Why? Because despite all the noise, you heard the faint cry of your infant, a sound that pierced through the pleasant cadence, calling for your attention.

Your mama's heart is so entwined with the needs of your baby, isn't it? In just this very way, your heart can also be attuned to the gentle whispers of the Holy Spirit. God doesn't always speak in thunderous declarations or dramatic displays. More often than not, He speaks in the quiet whispers of His Word, gently nudging us in the right direction.

Dear mama, today learn to cultivate that listening ear. Lean in close to the whispers of God's Spirit, for there lies the path to peace and guidance. As you spend time in His presence, let His voice become the melody that guides your steps and calms your fears. Trust in His leading, for He knows the way and will gently steer you toward His perfect will. In the midst of life's cacophony, may you find solace in the stillness of God's voice, guiding you with love and wisdom every step of the way.

Lord,

I'm listening.

Speak to me Your words of light and love.

Amen.

COMING HOME

Preserve me, O God,
for in you I take refuge.
PSALM 16:1 ESV

When the kids were very young, I used to watch the clock for the time of day when my husband would get home from work, and I could take a break from diapers and bottles and the exhaustion that parenting babies and young kids can bring. He'd say, "I'm home," and despite any problems we might have been experiencing, I'd heave a sigh of relief.

In many families, the words "I'm home" can instantly fill a space with warmth and joy. When a loved one has returned, the house almost seems to exhale with relief, eagerly awaiting a response. Yet for some, especially newly single parents, these homecomings are replaced with echoes of loneliness, leaving a void that seems impossible to fill.

Home is more than a place; it's a sanctuary where love and family envelop us like a comforting embrace. In the Bible, David understood this deeply. He often found solace in God, referring to Him as his "refuge." Through life's trials, David learned that he could always turn to God for safety and care, finding refuge in His unfailing love.

But what about those times when loss or broken relationships leave us feeling hollow inside? It's like a cavernous emptiness echoing in the depths of our soul. While reaching out to others may offer temporary relief, true restoration comes when we seek refuge in God. He alone has the power to breathe hope into our weary hearts, filling the emptiness with His boundless love and grace.

In today's digital age, it's easy to feel disconnected despite being constantly connected online. The longing for genuine face-to-face interaction persists, reminding us of our innate need for human connection. If you're grappling with a sense of emptiness today, try to get out in the community. Call a friend or meet a prayer partner for a cup of coffee. But more than this, like David did, remember that God is your ultimate Refuge. When you turn to Him, He opens His arms wide, welcoming you into His loving embrace. Make Him your safe haven and your constant companion in this journey called life!

Heavenly Father,

with You in my life, I know I am never alone.

Thank You that I am always at home with You.

Amen.

RENEWED STRENGTH

But those who hope in the Lord
will renew their strength.
They will soar on wings like eagles;
they will run and not grow weary,
they will walk and not faint.

ISAIAH 40:31 NIV

Are you feeling a bit worn out today? It happens, especially when life throws its usual whirlwind of busyness your way. Sometimes, in the midst of it all, our dreams can start to feel like distant memories, overshadowed by the demands of the daily grind.

But do you know what? You're not alone in feeling this way. Even in ancient times, people faced similar struggles. Take the people of Judah, for example. Seventy long years of captivity had left them feeling weary and disheartened. Yet, in the midst of their despair, the prophet Isaiah brought them a message of hope.

The prophet reminded them that God, their Creator, hadn't forgotten about them. How could He when He knows each and every one of His creations by name? It was a gentle nudge to shift their focus from their circumstances to the strength and power of God. Because when we fix our eyes on Him, we tap into a wellspring of divine strength and courage.

So when life starts to feel overwhelming, take a moment to pause and reconnect with the Source of all strength and renewal. Treat yourself to a little self-care, whether it's indulging in a luxurious bath or simply soaking in the beauty of a perfect sunset. Let the cares and the worries of the day melt away as you bask in the presence of God.

Single mama, you're stronger than you think, especially when you rely on the strength of your heavenly Father. Take heart, take a breath, and let His love and grace wash over you, refreshing your spirit and empowering you for the day ahead.

Lord,

I hope in You.

Thank You for renewing my strength this day.

Amen.

LEARNING TO THRIVE

My soul [my life, my very self]
is satisfied as with marrow and fatness, and
my mouth offers praises [to You] with joyful lips.
When I remember You on my bed,
I meditate and thoughtfully
focus on You in the night watches.

PSALM 63:5–6 AMP

You know, as a single mom, you're constantly nurturing and caring for those around you, much like a gardener must tend to all her plants. And just like those plants, you, too, deserve to thrive and flourish in your own life.

What does "thriving" look like for you? You might say, "Whatever it is, this isn't it!" Your definition of *thriving* will be as unique as you are. Sometimes it's about embracing adventure and spontaneity, while for other mamas, it might be about finding peace and stillness in the midst of life's chaos. Let me tell you, though, thriving doesn't always mean being constantly busy or productive. Sometimes it's simply about finding joy in the little moments, like snuggling up with a good book or taking a leisurely stroll with your kids.

Instead of getting caught up in the hustle and bustle

of life this week, why not pause and ask the Lord how He wants you to thrive? Trust me, He knows exactly what your soul needs to flourish. Maybe it involves carving out some quiet time for yourself, or perhaps it's finding joy in the everyday moments with your children.

Take a moment today to let God nurture your spirit and guide you toward a place of true flourishing. Whether it's through prayer, meditation, or simply enjoying the beauty of His creation, create space in your life for God to work His wonders in your heart.

Dear single mama, you're a beautiful, resilient soul, and you deserve to thrive in every sense of the word! So, take a deep breath, soak in the warmth of God's love, and embrace each moment as an opportunity to flourish in His grace.

Lord,

like a thirsty plant, I long to soak up Your presence. Teach me to thrive in the light of Your love today.

Amen.

A LIGHTER BURDEN

"Take My yoke upon you.
Let Me teach you,
because I am humble and gentle at heart,
and you will find rest for your souls.
For My yoke is easy to bear,
and the burden I give you is light."

MATTHEW 11:29–30

Have you ever found yourself in a rut, trying every trick in the book to solve a problem, only to feel like you're running on empty? It's tough, I know. But even when you feel like you've tried everything and come up short, there's still hope.

Jesus Himself promised that if you're feeling weary and worn out, He'll give you the rest and hope you so desperately need. Life has a way of piling on responsibilities, leaving you feeling like you're carrying the weight of the world on your shoulders. But Jesus offers a different kind of burden, one that's light and easy to bear.

Think of it like this: When you're feeling weighed down by life's demands, it's like being harnessed to a heavy yoke—or, for you and me, single mama, ten grocery bags filled with gallon jugs of milk that need to be carried up three flights of stairs! You may feel like they are dragging you down with every step you take. Jesus invites you to exchange that heavy burden for His own, one that's tailor-made to fit your shoulders perfectly.

When you find yourself at the end of your rope, feeling hopeless and out of options, it's time to hit the pause button and turn to Jesus. Take a break, indulge in something you love, and let go of the worries, just for a minute or two. A little rest and relaxation can work wonders for your soul.

You're not alone in this journey, single mama. Jesus is right there beside you, ready to help and lead you into a brighter tomorrow.

Lord,

my burdens seem so heavy at times.
Help me to release them to You
and rest in Your presence.

Amen.

THE
HUMBLE
WILL SEE
THEIR GOD
AT WORK
AND BE
GLAD.

LET ALL
WHO SEEK
GOD'S HELP
BE
ENCOURAGED.

Psalm 69:32

YOU'VE GOT THIS!

Now may our Lord Jesus Christ Himself and God our Father, who loved us and by His grace gave us eternal comfort and a wonderful hope, comfort you and strengthen you in every good thing you do and say.

2 THESSALONIANS 2:16–17

Ever have one of those days when it feels like the universe is conspiring against you? Your kids are in full-on meltdown mode, work is piling up, and the weight of your responsibilities feels like it's about to crush you. Nobody said single parenting was for the faint of heart!

No matter how rough today might be, tomorrow brings a brand-new dawn. Every tough night gives way to a fresh sunrise, and every frustrating day holds the promise of a peaceful evening. Even when it feels like the day is spiraling out of control, there's always the chance for a turnaround.

When God said His mercies are new every morning, He meant it. It's like clockwork, as dependable as the rising sun. His grace is more than enough to carry you through each day, no matter how rough it gets! Take peace in the knowledge that God specializes in fresh starts. His love for you knows no bounds, and His mercies are endless. Even if today feels like a total write-off, take heart—tomorrow is a blank slate, ready for you to start afresh.

Rest easy tonight, dear mama, knowing that tomorrow is a new day—a chance to start again, to embrace the beauty of a fresh start, and to walk hand in hand with the One who holds the universe in His hands. You've got this, Mama—and God's got you!

Dear Lord,

today has been a challenge, and I have felt so overwhelmed. Still, I know You are working in my life—sustaining me and giving me strength. Thank You for the goodness You always display in my life—each and every day. With Your help, I know I've got this!

Amen.

DANGER AND OPPORTUNITY

The righteous person faces many troubles, but the LORD comes to the rescue each time.

PSALM 34:19

During my college years, I did some traveling in Southeast Asia, and while doing so, I picked up a bit of the Chinese language. Come to find out, the old saying *is* true: in Chinese, the word for *crisis* is made up of two characters—one representing danger and the other representing opportunity. During that fun and exciting time of life, "danger" and "opportunity" seemed exhilarating as I was eager to explore new people and places and discover all the world had to offer.

Now, as a single mama, "danger" seems a bit more ominous. Falling behind on the car payment or mortgage? That's a different kind of danger altogether from hiking up Machu Picchu. Still, the Chinese characters I learned so long ago remain a beautiful reminder that even in the midst of the dangers we face—mundane or exhilarating—there's always the potential for something good to emerge.

Here's the thing: No one is immune to hardship. We all face various dangers, disappointments, and losses at some point in our lives. But even in our darkest moments, God has a way of shedding light on our paths, turning our trials into triumphs.

When you face a crisis head-on, it becomes an opportunity for growth and transformation. Maybe that late mortgage payment is an opportunity for you to trust God for greater provision. It's a chance to draw from your inner strength and courage while you allow the Lord to guide your steps. And as you focus on finding solutions to the challenges you face, you'll discover just how resilient and capable you truly are when you are trusting in Him.

Lord,

You give me opportunities each day
to grow in my faith and learn to trust You more.
Help me to take advantage of each of these situations
and view them as a chance to grow closer to You.

Amen.

THE NEVER-ENDING TO-DO LIST

Therefore since we are surrounded
by such a great cloud of witnesses,
let us throw off everything that hinders
and the sin that so easily entangles.
And let us run with perseverance
the race marked out for us.

HEBREWS 12:1 NIV

Have you ever had one of those days when it feels like nothing goes according to plan? You had a list a mile long—work projects, errands, chores, family obligations—but somehow, *none of it* got done! And now you're left feeling discouraged and exhausted at bedtime, wondering where the day went.

Here's the thing, though, dear mama: It's okay to have days like that! Sometimes our expectations of ourselves can be sky-high, leaving us feeling overwhelmed and stuck in a never-ending cycle of disappointment. But guess what? It's okay to hit the pause button and say, "I'll try again tomorrow."

Each of us is only human, and that includes you! We can't do it all. And that's perfectly okay. God promises to take care of us, even when our to-do lists remain unfinished.

His love for us isn't contingent on our productivity or accomplishments. So why not take a deep breath and let go of your unrealistic expectations?

Instead of beating yourself up over what didn't get done today, shift your perspective. Look at your day through God's eyes. His expectations for us are rooted in love and grace, not in a never-ending list of things to get done (that you will probably have to do again next week). Take a moment right now to surrender your plans to Him and ask for His guidance to look toward tomorrow as a brand-new day, filled with possibility!

Lord,

I surrender my to-do list to You today.
I admit it can be a tyrannical master at times;
I would rather serve only You.
Help me to set my priorities according to Your will.
I give my plans to You today.

Amen.

EAGER ANTICIPATION

And I am certain that God,
who began the good work within you,
will continue His work until it is finally finished
on the day when Christ Jesus returns.

PHILIPPIANS 1:6

It's really impossible to live without hope, isn't it? Hope is like a beacon of light on the darkest of days, guiding us through the ups and downs of life. And as single moms, hope often becomes our lifeline, doesn't it? It can truly be our anchor in the storm—especially when it's a hope based on God's good work in our lives.

Real hope isn't just about wishing for something better; it's about *eagerly anticipating* the good things that lie ahead. (When was the last time you "eagerly anticipated" something—other than a new haircut or a nap?) Just like kids who count down the days until Christmas (sometimes starting in September!) or adults who eagerly await a vacation, we, too, can find solace in the promise of better days to come.

Let's be real, though. Life sure has a way of being unpredictable at times, squashing our hopes and dreams in the process. Maybe you've found yourself grappling with disappointment lately, wondering if your dreams will ever come true. Or perhaps you're somewhere in between: holding on to hope while navigating the challenges of being a single mama.

Here's the beautiful truth: God sees you. He knows your past, your present, and your future. He knows every hope, every dream, and every desire of your heart. And the best part? He's not just a bystander in your story; He's an active participant, working behind the scenes to bring about His perfect plan for your life.

Instead of placing your hope in the uncertain things of this world, why not anchor it in the unwavering certainty of God's love and faithfulness? Trust me—He'll never let you down, His promises are as sure as the rising sun, and His plans for you are greater than anything you could ever imagine.

Lord,

I want to do more than just hope
in the temporal things of this world—
I want to eagerly anticipate the good things
You have for my life. Help me to trust
in Your promises this day.

Amen.

CHOOSING GRACE

Bear with each other and forgive one another if any of you has a grievance against someone. Forgive as the Lord forgave you.

COLOSSIANS 3:13 NIV

G*race* is such a beautiful word. It means the "unmerited favor of God." I love this word so much that I named my second child, my precious daughter, Gracie—and she has truly been a gift of grace to me.

The grace of God is what we need the most, isn't it, single mama? It's like a soothing balm for the soul, offering comfort and healing in the midst of life's challenges. And as a single mom, you know that grace is an invaluable tool in your tool kit for navigating the ups and downs of everyday life.

You see, when someone mistreats us or rubs us the wrong way, our first instinct might be to complain or vent our frustrations. And you know what? I get it—sometimes letting off some steam feels good in the moment. But more often than not, it leaves us feeling even more frustrated than before.

Instead of getting caught up in a cycle of complaining, why not choose grace instead? It takes courage to turn the other cheek, to offer forgiveness when others have wronged us. And trust me, it's not always easy. But when we choose grace, we open the door to healing and reconciliation.

Don't get me wrong—there are times when it's important to address issues head-on, to speak up for ourselves, and to advocate for our children's well-being. But there are also moments when all we need to do is extend a little grace, to offer a listening ear or a kind word instead of lashing out in anger.

Dear mama, let's choose grace today. Let's be the light in a world that can sometimes feel dark and unforgiving. And as we do, may we find healing, peace, and strength in the boundless grace of our loving heavenly Father.

Heavenly Father,

You are so good, and Your grace is truly amazing! Thank You for shining Your grace through my life and allowing me to share Your light with others who also need Your love.

Amen.

LETTING GO OF THE MESS

"There is only one thing
worth being concerned about.
Mary has discovered it, and
it will not be taken away from her."

LUKE 10:42

Has your "mess threshold" ever just hit the roof? Sometimes it seems like one minute, everything is "under control"—as much as it can be, at least—and then, within mere moments, chaos erupts. The baby throws a bowl of Cheerios, the dog pukes, and someone has tracked mud from the backyard all over the carpet.

"Argh! I don't have time for this," we say to ourselves, so *many* times a day. Or "Ugh, not again. *Another* mess?" Busyness can consume the life of the single mama, always vying for our attention and pulling us in a million different directions. It can sometimes feel like there just aren't enough hours in the day to get everything done.

Here's the thing, though: Our schedules are a reflection of our priorities. Every choice we make, every item we put on our calendar, shapes the way we spend our time. And the question we may need to ask ourselves is this: Are we making room for God in the midst of our busyness?

Take Mary and Martha, for example. They were friends of Jesus, and when He came to visit, Martha was busy bustling around, trying to make everything perfect. Meanwhile, Mary chose to simply sit at Jesus' feet, soaking in His presence. It's a reminder that sometimes, in the middle of all the chaos, we need to pause and make time for the things that truly matter.

Making God a priority doesn't mean neglecting your responsibilities or abandoning your commitments. It's all about finding balance and perspective, putting Him first and trusting that everything else will fall into place.

If you find yourself feeling overwhelmed by your schedule today, it might be time to take a step back and reevaluate your priorities. Is there something you can let go of to make more room for God in your life? Can you carve out a few moments today to simply sit at His feet and bask in His love?

God,

sometimes the day seems like it's filled with one mess after another, and I'm tempted to take on a "Martha" attitude. Help me to keep a tender spirit like Mary's, open to Your voice and eager to bask in Your presence.

Amen.

RENEWED HOPE

After Job had prayed for his friends,
the LORD restored his fortunes and
gave him twice as much as he had before.
JOB 42:10 NIV

Heartbreak. Shattered dreams. They can make life seem like you are walking through a storm with no end in sight, wondering why it has to be so hard. It's okay, though—to ask questions, to wonder why life is so tough sometimes.

Take Job, for example. He faced more problems all at once than most of us face in a lifetime. He lost everything—his family, his wealth, his health—and in the midst of it all, he couldn't help but ask why. Why was he suffering? Why did God allow it to happen?

Sometimes the answers we seek aren't the ones we receive. Instead of giving Job a direct answer, God responded with more questions. He asked Job where he was when the world was created, reminding him of His own infinite power and wisdom. That realization humbled Job, reminding him that even in the midst of his pain, God was still in control. Despite the heartbreak, despite the shattered dreams, God had the power to make everything new again—and He did.

When life hands you unexpected disappointments and challenges, when you find yourself asking why, try shifting your focus. Instead of dwelling on the whys, trust in God's goodness and find comfort in His presence. Even when we don't understand why certain things happen, we can trust that God is with us, comforting us, strengthening us, and giving us renewed hope.

Sure, life here on earth is certainly filled with suffering and pain, but that's not the end of the story. In heaven, there will be no more tears, no more pain—just endless joy and peace in the presence of our heavenly Father. So hold on to hope, dear mama, knowing that even in the darkest moments, God is with you, walking alongside you every step of the way. As you trust in Him and find comfort in His love, you will discover a renewed sense of hope in the middle of all that you face this day.

Lord,

I bring my heartache and disappointment to You. Thank You for Your comfort, Your peace, and the hope that better days are ahead.

Amen.

THE BEAUTY OF UNEXPECTED MOMENTS

Thank God for this gift
too wonderful for words!
II CORINTHIANS 9:15

My phone buzzed with a text, and I looked down. The meeting I was rushing to get ready for had just been postponed. First there was a twinge of frustration—I had worked hard to prepare, after all—but then, a sense of delight. I could take an unexpected breather in my schedule, maybe browse through that cute little thrift shop I never had the chance to visit, or leisurely stroll through the grocery store instead of spinning through it like Taz from *Looney Tunes*, looking for the right brand of mayo, per my usual form.

What about you? Have you ever had one of those moments when your plans suddenly got canceled and you found yourself with an unexpected opening in your day? It's like a little gift from above, a Godwink, a chance to catch your breath and take a step back from the hustle and bustle of everyday life. Here's the thing, though: When those moments come along, do you feel the temptation to fill them with the very next thing on your to-do list? I sure have. But what if, instead of rushing to fill the void, we took a moment to pause and ask ourselves: Do I *really* need to do anything right now?

Maybe this is truly an opportunity to hit the reset button for a moment, to take a much-needed break and rejuvenate your weary soul. Maybe it's a chance to spend a little extra quality time with your loved ones, your kids, to make memories that will last a lifetime.

When our schedules unexpectedly open up, it's easy to fall into the trap of treating our lives like a series of never-ending checklists. But what if we approached our calendars with a more human, less frantic mindset? What if we allowed ourselves to simply *be*, to savor the gift of unexpected time? After all, life is meant to be lived, not rushed through. So take a deep breath, dear mama, and let yourself enjoy the beauty of unexpected moments.

Lord,

thank You for reminding me
of Your love and care for me,
even in the middle of my busy days.
You always know what I need!

Amen.

MAKE TIME TO LAUGH!

A time to weep and a time to laugh,
a time to mourn and a time to dance.
ECCLESIASTES 3:4 NIV

Laughter. It's like a ray of sunshine on even the gloomiest of days, brightening our spirits and filling our hearts with joy. As a single mama, laughter can become our very lifeline in the family, our secret weapon for getting us and our kids through the ups and downs of daily life. Whenever I am down about anything, I find myself thinking of my son's easy laugh or my daughter's mischievous, dimpled grin. Even as they are growing older, they still laugh easily—and wholeheartedly—at anything, *anything*, that seems funny!

When was the last time *you* had a good belly laugh with your kiddos? Laughter should always have a place in our lives, especially during those precious years with your kids. It's a reminder to slow down, to cherish the little moments, and to find joy in the everyday situations that we face. If you find yourself feeling overwhelmed by the busyness of life today, it might be time to take a step back and take a breather. Your own well-being and the happiness of your family are more important than getting everything done immediately.

Happy is the mama who lets laughter be her guide, so fill your home with silly jokes, funny stories, and laughter-filled moments. Set traditions that bring fun and joy into each day—dinnertime cooking dance-off, anyone?—because those will bring the memories that last. At the end of the day, it's the moments of laughter and joy that truly matter. They are the glue that will hold your family together through even the darkest of times, the fuel that will keep each of you going, and the memories you will cherish for a lifetime. Start today to make laughter the soundtrack of your family's life!

Lord,

thank You for the joy of a life filled with love and laughter and You. No matter what else is going on, I choose to cultivate a positive spirit and provide a happy home for my family.

Amen.

THE SAFETY NET OF COMMUNITY

Share each other's burdens,
and in this way obey the law of Christ.
GALATIANS 6:2

Financially, the first year I was single "ate my lunch." Lawyers and court filings for custody took nearly all my money, and it was tear-out-your-hair difficult to keep the lights on, a roof over our heads, and food on the table. But I learned a great lesson in that early-on time: I didn't have to do it all on my own. So many friends and family members were truly willing to help—right down to my new neighbors, who came over and mowed the overgrown yard of the house we were moving into.

Having a community of people around you is like having a safety net of love and support that can catch you when life tries to knock you down. And as a single mom, having a strong community on which to lean can make all the difference in the world.

Think about it—whom do you turn to when you need a shoulder to cry on, a listening ear, or just a helping hand? Those people, my friend, are your community. They're the ones who have got your back, who will drop everything to lend a hand or offer a word of encouragement.

Being vulnerable isn't always easy, especially in a world that often tells us to tough it out on our own. But here's the thing: when you open up and let people in, you'll be amazed at the love and support that may come in return.

So don't be afraid to reach out when you need help. Whether you have just had surgery and you could use some meals, or you're struggling with a tempestuous two-year-old, or you're feeling overwhelmed by the loss of a job or a lack of finances—your community can be there for you. All you have to do is ask.

And you know what? When you're feeling rested and ready to pay it forward, be sure to do just that. Because true community isn't just about receiving—it's about giving back too. It's about lifting each other up, sharing each other's burdens, and walking the journey of life together.

Here's to community, dear mama. May we always be willing to lean on each other, to share in each other's joys and sorrows, and to point each other to the true Source of help and comfort.

Lord,

thank You for other people whom You have placed in my life, who graciously show me Your love. Help me to be a blessing to others in this same way, showing Your care and concern to those who need it.

Amen.

HIS UNFORGETTABLE WORKS OF SURPASSING WONDER

REVEAL
HIS GRACE
AND
TENDER
MERCY.

Psalm 111:4 TPT

MOM GUILT

And God raised us up with Christ and seated us with Him in the heavenly realms in Christ Jesus, in order that in the coming ages He might show the incomparable riches of His grace, expressed in His kindness to us in Christ Jesus.

EPHESIANS 2:6–7 NIV

I will be the first to admit it—as a mom, I mess up. A lot. There are days when I think I've got this whole parenting thing down, and then there are days when I could sure use a do-over! The beautiful part is that I'm not alone. None of us are. We all have our moments of stumbling, of falling short. That's okay! Because in those moments, we have a loving Father who is ready and waiting to scoop us up in His arms and remind us that we are forgiven and loved beyond measure.

We all know the drill—feeling guilty just comes with the territory of being human sometimes. And if you're a single mama, trying to navigate through life, it's easy to let guilt find its way into your mind and heart. I'm not talking about your conscience, the Holy Spirit, when He comes to nudge you and tell you which way to go. I'm talking about the toxic kind of guilt—the feeling that you've done too many things wrong to ever get back on the right track, or that you are failing your kids, or that you should have made better choices in your life.

Here's the kicker: When guilt starts to constantly hang around like a gloomy cloud, day in and day out, it can take its toll. Suddenly we feel like we are drowning in shame, like we are not worthy of love or forgiveness. There is good news, though: God doesn't want us living under a cloud of shame. Not at all! He's all about second chances, about wiping the slate clean and saying, "Dear daughter, you're forgiven. Let's learn from this and move forward, shall we?"

Let's ditch the guilt and the shame today, single mama! Instead, let's focus on seeking God's grace, on moving forward with hope and determination. We're worthy! We're loved. And we've got a whole lot of living left to do!

Lord,

today I set aside the past
and any toxic guilt I'm feeling.
I know that is not from You!
Thank You for Your grace and the chance to
move forward into a better day tomorrow.

Amen.

"NOT FAIR!"

He is the Rock; His deeds are perfect.
Everything He does is just and fair.
He is a faithful God who does no wrong;
how just and upright He is!
DEUTERONOMY 32:4

When the kids were little, they sure did fight a lot. My son was pretty even-natured, but my daughter had an innate sense of right and wrong—and it was often the hill she'd prefer to die upon. I'll never forget the day when my sweet Gracie, with all the drama of a little diva, yelled at the top of her lungs, "That's not fair!" Who knows now what it was about—the point was that she felt wronged, and she wanted to let the world know about it!

Fairness. It's an elusive concept that can trip up even the tiniest of tots. Maybe my daughter's words sound familiar to you because you've heard your own kids shout them out. Or maybe they're familiar because you hear them echoing in your own heart.

Fairness isn't just a kid thing. It's something we grown-ups grapple with too. And as single moms, some days it seems we've got a front-row seat at the unfairness show. Whether it's struggling to make ends meet, facing judgment from others, or simply trying to shield our kids from life's harsh realities, we know all too well the sting of injustice.

Here's the silver lining, though: fairness isn't the be-all, end-all. Not by a long shot. Because when we zoom out and take a look at the bigger picture, we can see something even more powerful at play: love. Yep, you heard me: love trumps fairness every time. So when my kiddos found themselves in a time-out showdown, we didn't just focus on who was right or wrong. The more important lesson to learn wasn't "What's fair?" but "What's the loving thing to do here?"

You may feel unfairly treated today, maybe by your ex-spouse, your ex-in-laws, people at church, or your boss at work. Let love be your powerful secret sauce that can turn your potential meltdown into a teachable moment. Extend grace and forgiveness, even when it feels like the scales of justice are tipped against you. Embrace the beauty of love instead. Because when we lead with love, we're not just teaching our kids a lesson about fairness, we're showing them what it means to live like Jesus.

Heavenly Father,

You are fair and just. I trust You with the parts of my life that seem "unfair," and I choose to focus instead on Your love and grace this day.

Amen.

THE WIDOW'S REWARD

So she did as Elijah said, and she and Elijah and her family continued to eat for many days. There was always enough flour and olive oil left in the containers, just as the LORD had promised through Elijah.

I KINGS 17:15–16

Single motherhood isn't some newfangled concept; did you know it's been around since the times of the Bible? Believe it or not, God has always had a bit of a soft spot for moms who had to fly solo. Let's take a look at one in the Old Testament book of I Kings, a widow who lived in a town called Zarephath. She had lost her husband, and she was trying to raise her only son alone, just trying to make ends meet and keep food on the table. Unfortunately, a famine hit her land and her village hard. So, when the prophet Elijah showed up on her doorstep asking her for food, she didn't really feel like rolling out the welcome mat. No, she was barely scraping by, wondering how she was going to feed her own kiddo, let alone this unexpected guest.

But here is where things got interesting. Instead of giving in to despair (like I might do, if I had company and an empty pantry), this brave mama decided to take a leap of faith. She dug deep, found that last ounce of trust in

God she had, and decided to share her meager provisions with Elijah. And you know what? God didn't let her down! Her act of faith triggered a miracle, and suddenly she had enough food to go around, with plenty to spare.

Today, dear mama, you may be thinking your own situation feels impossible. *How could God possibly turn things around for me like that?* you might be thinking. Well, let me remind you: God specializes in turning the impossible into the miraculous. Just like He did for the widow of Zarephath, He's ready and waiting to swoop in and rescue you from whatever mess you find yourself in.

So, when you're feeling weary and when you are at the end of your rope, remember this: God hasn't forgotten about you! He's got a plan; He's got provision; He's got a miracle with your name on it. Keep the faith, keep trusting Him, and step back and watch as He works mighty wonders in your life.

Lord,

help me to have the faith and trust in You
that the widow of Zarephath displayed.
Even when I'm at the end of my rope,
I'll keep holding on and listening for Your voice.
You will never let me down!

Amen.

LOST IN THE DESERT

And the angel also said,
"You are now pregnant and will give birth to a son.
You are to name him Ishmael (which means 'God hears'),
for the Lord has heard your cry of distress."
GENESIS 16:11

If you've ever felt "lost in the desert" as a single mom, you're not alone. Single parenthood *can* feel like a parched desert sometimes, can't it? A desert of provision, a desert of loneliness, a desert of spiritual and emotional thirst. It's a good thing God knows how to take care of single moms who find themselves there!

You may remember the story of Abraham and Sarah and their struggle to see the fulfillment of the promise from God for a son. In this story, we tend to paint Hagar as the villain. She was the one who got pregnant and had a baby by Abraham, right? But let's take a closer look. You see, Hagar wasn't exactly "living the dream." No, she was caught smack-dab in the middle of a messy situation, forced to do things she never signed up for.

Imagine being in her shoes. She was forced into a relationship she didn't ask for, then forced to bear a child. Then, when things got tough in the family dynamics, she was tossed out into the desert with that child, with nothing but a bottle of water and a prayer. Talk about a rough hand dealt!

But even in the middle of the desert, even when all hope seemed lost, God showed up for Hagar. In that barren and desolate place, He heard Hagar's cries, He saw her pain, and He had mercy on her and her son.

There have been many times in my own life when I've felt like I'm wandering in the desert, no relief in sight. Maybe you're feeling overwhelmed, without hope or a plan, no one left to turn to. But the beautiful thing is, dear mama, even in the desert, God is right there by your side. He's listening, He's waiting, and He's ready to turn your desert into a garden of blessings.

If you are in a desert today—of any sort—take heart. You're not alone, and you're not forgotten. Go ahead and cry out to God like Hagar did. Pour out your heart, lay your burdens at His feet, and watch as He turns your desert into a place of abundance and joy. Trust me: He's got this—and He's got you!

Heavenly Father,

just as You saw Hagar and cared for her and her child in the desert, I know You will do the same for me. Thank You for Your unending love.

Amen.

A DAUGHTER OF GOD

I pray that out of His glorious riches
He may strengthen you with power
through His Spirit in your inner being.

EPHESIANS 3:16 NIV

Remember the story of Cinderella? She was mistreated by her stepmother and stepsisters, forced to labor in impossible circumstances—until a prince finally came to her rescue. I always wondered where her father was in that story. Surely a loving parent would never want his daughter treated in such a way!

Think about it for real, though. Imagine going through a day with one of your precious kiddos. Now, instead of showering them with love and kindness, you're laying the pressure on thick. You're waking them up at the crack of dawn, forcing them to skip breakfast, and piling on impossible tasks like there's no tomorrow. Would you ever treat your child like that? Of course not!

Here's an entirely different thought on the matter: if we wouldn't treat our kids like that, why in the world do we tend to treat *ourselves* that way? This may be a tough question, but it's worth pondering.

Here's the thing: self-care isn't just a luxury; it's

a necessity. And as single moms, it's all too easy to put our own needs on the back burner, isn't it? Here's a little reminder for you: you are just as deserving of love, kindness, and rest as anyone else.

So, here's a challenge for today: Treat yourself like the precious child of God that you are. He's your Father—and you're no Cinderella. Relax those sky-high expectations, show yourself some grace, and take a breather when life starts to feel overwhelming. Because here is the beautiful truth: God sees you, He loves you, and He wants nothing more than for you to thrive, even in the challenges you face.

So go ahead, Mama, take a moment for yourself today. Whether it's a bubble bath you need or a walk in the park or just a few quiet moments with your Bible and Jesus, prioritize your well-being and watch as joy and peace flood into your life. You deserve it, Mama. Go ahead—treat yourself like the precious treasure you are!

Lord,

at times, I feel like Cinderella, working so hard to get everything done. Help me to remember that You are a loving Father who does not require that of me, and that Jesus, my Prince, has already come to my rescue. Thank You for saving me!

Amen.

THE WEB OF GUILT

May the Lord smile on you
and be gracious to you.
May the Lord show you His favor
and give you His peace.
NUMBERS 6:25–26

Maybe if I'd just tried harder . . .

That thought still tries to come in my head when I think about the divorce—especially when I consider what I'd truly wanted in life for my kids.

What about you? Do you ever deal with the pesky little thing called *guilt*? Whether it's mommy guilt, work guilt, or just plain life guilt, it seems like we women have a knack for beating ourselves up over the smallest slipups—or the biggest ones—or any ones in between.

It's time to cut ourselves some slack—at least on the things that don't really matter. God is not up in heaven keeping score, tallying up all our mistakes, frowning when we get even the most minor parts of our days all wrong. Nope, He's all about grace, love, and forgiveness. And He's got plenty to spare.

If you've found yourself tangled up in a web of guilt today, take a deep breath and let it go. Seriously, Mama, you don't need to keep replaying those mistakes or dwelling on the bad moments. Even the questions you have about your past—you can lay those at His feet. God sees you, He loves you, and He's got your back, no matter what.

Here's the challenge for us as single moms today: Let's give ourselves a healthy dose of grace. Instead of dwelling on what went wrong, focus on what went right. Remind yourself that you are loved, cherished, and forgiven—flaws and all.

If self-condemning thoughts start creeping in, try to see yourself through the eyes of your loving heavenly Father. Because trust me, He sees you as His precious child, worthy of love, acceptance, and grace.

Go ahead, Mama, give yourself permission to let go of the guilt and embrace the freedom that comes from knowing you are covered with grace. Rest in the knowledge that God removes your sins from you gladly and willingly—the very moment you ask. You've got this, Mama. As you bask in the glow of God's love and forgiveness, remember that you deserve it. He sent His Son to die for you—there's no need to experience the guilt any longer, once you bring it all to Him.

God,

thank You for Your grace that covers me and all my mistakes. I embrace Your freedom today and choose to walk in Your love.

Amen.

REST FOR THE WEARY, PEACE FOR THE WORN OUT

"I am leaving you with a gift—
peace of mind and heart.
And the peace I give is
a gift the world cannot give.
So don't be troubled or afraid."

JOHN 14:27

When Jesus said He would give us peace, He wasn't kidding. He meant every word of it.

Think for a minute about what that really means. Right in the middle of our crazy, chaotic lives, Jesus extends His invitation: "Come to Me, all you who are tired and worn out, and I'll give you peace" (Matthew 11:28 paraphrase). Do you qualify as someone who is "tired and worn out"? I know I sure do—most days! Does that promise sound too good to be true? It's not. It's the real deal.

Jesus isn't in the business of making empty promises. He's all about delivering on His Word, and He's got a track record that speaks for itself. So, when He says He will give us peace, you better believe He means it!

You might be wondering if asking God for peace in

the middle of your “minor” problems each day might seem like a big request. Does God really have time for our little challenges and issues? Let me set the record straight: God is just waiting for you to come to Him and ask. He is waiting for the chance to shower you with His peace, His love, and His grace.

God longs for weary moms to come to Him with anything on their hearts. He wants us to be free from anxiety, fear, and worry. He wants us to enjoy life, to savor every precious moment with our kiddos—without constantly feeling like we’re drowning in a sea of stress.

Take heart, dear mama. Even when the world feels like it may be spinning out of control, remember this: Jesus promised us peace, and He’s not about to go back on His word. Lean into His promises, soak in His presence, and watch as He fills your heart with a peace that surpasses all understanding. With Jesus by your side, Mama, you’ve got all the peace you’ll ever need.

Lord,

thank You for Your peace
in the middle of my semi-chaotic life.
My heart can rest in You.

Amen.

ASKING FOR HELP

Let's see how inventive we can be
in encouraging love and helping out,
not avoiding worshiping together as some do
but spurring each other on,
especially as we see the big Day approaching.

HEBREWS 10:25 THE MESSAGE

Asking for help is rarely easy. Our society tells us that we should be able to handle everything all on our own, right? We look around and see these "superwomen" who seem to have it all together, and we can't help but feel a twinge of envy.

But asking for help isn't a sign of weakness; it's actually an act of courage. It takes real guts to admit when we are struggling, to open up, and to be vulnerable with those around us. But trust me, it's worth it.

When we are willing to ask for help, we create space for authentic connections to blossom. We give others permission to let down their guard, to be real about their own struggles. And let's be honest—wouldn't you rather surround yourself with people who are willing to show their true selves, flaws and all, than people who are just pretending to have it all together?

Consider reaching out to someone in your circle today

and ask for some help. It could be your best friend, a neighbor, a family member, or a coworker—whoever you feel comfortable with. Don't be ashamed! Chances are, they've been where you are, and they'll be more than happy to lend a hand. And who knows? Your willingness to ask for help just might inspire others to do the same. You could be the catalyst for a whole new culture of vulnerability and support in your community. Go ahead and take that first step—you've got this, and you're not alone.

Lord,

help me to set aside my pride today
and ask for help from others when I need it.
Thank You for always being there for me.

Amen.

REMEMBERING YOUR PURPOSE

The Lord will fulfill his purpose for me;
your steadfast love, O Lord, endures forever.
Do not forsake the work of your hands.

PSALM 138:8 ESV

Look around at the incredible world that God has created! Have you ever stopped to think about it? From the majestic sun that warms the earth to the vast oceans teeming with life, every single thing has a purpose in this world.

Consider the seashell, for example. Picture yourself strolling along the beach with your kids, sand bucket in hand, on the hunt for treasures. And when you spot that glimmer of color peeking out from the sand, your little one rushes over to scoop up that tiny shell. It's a small reminder of God's creativity and purpose in all things.

You see, each seashell was once a home for a tiny sea creature. But even after the creature has moved on, the shell remains, a testament to God's handiwork and the fulfillment of its purpose. And guess what? Just like those seashells, you and I were created with a purpose too.

As single moms, it's so easy to get caught up in the busyness of life, isn't it? There are a million things vying for our attention, pulling us in a million different directions. But right in the middle of the chaos, God sees you. He knows you. And He created you with a purpose in mind.

So take a deep breath, Mama, and let this truth sink in: Everything God has made—including you—has a purpose. And He will fulfill that purpose in His perfect timing. Rest in that amazing truth, let it fill you with hope, and trust that God is at work, even in the midst of your busiest days. You've got this, Mama! And God's got you.

Lord,

I know You have a good purpose for me
and Your promises give me hope today.
Help me remember that, no matter
how busy I feel or what situations I face,
You are working out Your purpose in my life.

Amen.

LET GO OF THE HUSTLE

Even so, I have noticed one thing,
at least, that is good.
It is good for people to eat, drink,
and enjoy their work under the sun
during the short life God has given them,
and to accept their lot in life.

ECCLESIASTES 5:18

Most single mamas are not slackers. I have always been a super-hard worker—from keeping my grades up in high school to working multiple jobs to put myself through college and graduate school debt-free and with straight As, to starting my own business, and so on, and so on. But single motherhood has been one of the biggest challenges of my life!

A strong work ethic is a fantastic quality to have. And we mamas want our kiddos to grow up knowing the value of hard work. But here's the thing: sometimes that strong work ethic can start working against us.

Picture this: You're hustling day in and day out, trying to juggle a million different things at once. Sound familiar? It's so easy to get caught up in the hustle, to push ourselves to the limit in pursuit of perfection. But the truth is, God never intended for us to burn ourselves out. Sure, He does call us to work hard, to give our best in everything we do. But He also wants us to take care of ourselves, to prioritize our health and well-being as a matter of actual importance. When we are running on empty, when we are stretched too thin, we've got nothing left to give to the people who matter the most: our kiddos, our family, our friends.

Take a step back today and just admit that you can't do it all. It's okay to ask for help, to take a break, to give yourself some much-needed rest. After all, even God took a break when He was creating the world, didn't He? Whether it's a weekend staycation or simply taking a day off to recharge, give yourself permission to follow God's example and get a little rest. You'll come back feeling so much more refreshed and rejuvenated, ready to get back in the game and tackle whatever life throws your way.

God,

I know You have called us to work hard to care for our families and meet our responsibilities, but You also call us to rest. Help me to remember that fact in the middle of my busy day. When I hear Your voice calling me to step away and recharge my body and spirit, I will listen.

Amen.

MAY THE GOD
OF HOPE
FILL YOU
WITH ALL
JOY AND
PEACE AS YOU
TRUST IN HIM,

SO THAT YOU MAY OVERFLOW WITH HOPE BY THE POWER OF THE HOLY SPIRIT.

Romans 15:13 NIV

HE KNOWS YOUR NEEDS

And my God will supply every need of yours according to his riches in glory in Christ Jesus.

PHILIPPIANS 4:19 ESV

Finances can be such a major source of stress in the life of a single parent—especially when there is sooooo much more month left than money. Have you recently prayed as you swiped your credit card at the grocery store that it wouldn't get declined? It can be such a challenge to meet your kids' needs on one source of income if your children's father isn't chipping in. You may be clipping coupons, picking up odd jobs the best you can, maybe even working multiple jobs just to make ends meet. And yet, no matter how hard you work, it still feels like you're barely keeping your head above water.

Even in the midst of the financial struggle, dear mama, God sees you. He knows every bill that's due, every upcoming repair that will need to be made, every expense that is looming on the horizon. He knows it all, and He stands ready and willing to help.

Take a deep breath, Mama, and let that truth sink in. The same God who formed the very air you breathe, who knows every hair on your head, He knows your needs, and He promises to provide for you and your family. That's truly amazing, when you think about it.

Cling to God's promises today. Even if your bank account looks bleak, even if the bills keep piling up, rest in the provision of the cross. Trust that God is at work, even in the middle of your financial struggles. He will never leave you nor forsake you—with Him, you will have all the provision you need.

Lord,

I bring my bills, my grocery list,
all my needs to You today.
I know You know these needs even before I do.
I look to You as my Source.
Please continue to meet the needs of me
and my family as we trust in You.

Amen.

WHO ARE YOU?

For we are God's handiwork,
created in Christ Jesus to do good works,
which God prepared in advance for us to do.
EPHESIANS 2:10 NIV

Dear single mama, can we take a moment to celebrate . . . YOU? Seriously, give yourself a round of applause, because guess what? You are amazing. Yes, I'm talking about you, Mom: the accountant, the teacher, the nurse, the dishwasher, the taxi driver, the cook, the laundry lady, and the housekeeper—all rolled into one! You're not just one thing; you're a whole bunch of incredible things wrapped up in one awesome package called Mom.

Think about it a little further: You're not just a mom. You're also a sister, an aunt, a friend, a daughter. You're gentle and loyal, feisty and funny, intelligent and strong. You're adventurous, thoughtful, energetic, and totally unique. You're you!

But even though you're all these amazing things, you might not always feel so capable, right? You might feel weak, discouraged, overwhelmed, or even angry. You might wish you had a different life entirely on some really awful days. But no matter what your circumstances say, you're still you—and there's no one else like you in the entire world.

Here's the challenge for you today: Take some time to really get to know yourself. Think about what makes you who you are, what makes you unique. Connect with your authentic self and stop trying to be someone you're not. Because here's the truth: God created you exactly as you are, with all your quirks and flaws and strengths. And He thinks you're pretty amazing!

So, go ahead, Mama, embrace yourself. Celebrate all that makes you who you are—a beloved daughter of God, fearfully and wonderfully made. Every time you start to criticize yourself, ask your Maker for a little perspective. You'll find more rest and peace in embracing your true self, just as God created you to be.

Heavenly Father,

thank You for making me me.
Help me to see myself through Your eyes
and with Your grace, no matter what
"hat" I am wearing this day.

Amen.

JESUS' REST

Then, because so many people
were coming and going that
they did not even have a chance to eat,
He said to them,
"Come with Me by yourselves
to a quiet place and get some rest."
MARK 6:31 NIV

Rest? Time to kick back, relax, and recharge those batteries? Who has time for that? Between work, kids, and all the other things life throws our way, it can feel like there's never a spare moment to just sit back and breathe.

But resting isn't just a luxury; it's a necessity. Giving yourself permission to rest isn't something to feel guilty about; it's something to celebrate. Because here's the truth: when you take time to rest, you're not just doing yourself a favor, you're doing your whole family a favor! Are you at your best when you're worn out? Can you really finish all the tasks you need to get done when you're exhausted? Even if you can, can you maintain a good attitude while you do?

Even Jesus Himself knew the importance of rest. The very Son of God took time to kick back and relax with His disciples. He knew that in order for Him to minister effectively to others, He needed to keep up His own physical strength. The same goes for you, dear mama.

Today, look for some pockets of rest in your schedule. Whether it's taking a few moments to just breathe deeply as you pause in the driveway before going into the house, or getting to bed a few minutes earlier tonight, do whatever it takes to prioritize getting the rest you need. Trust me—you'll thank yourself for it later.

Remember, rest isn't just a luxury; it's a gift from God. Embrace it. Enjoy it. And know that by taking care of yourself, you're not just doing yourself a favor; you're honoring the body and soul that God has given to you.

Jesus,

when You call me to come away
with You to rest, I will listen and obey.
Thank You for Your care for me.

Amen.

"COME HERE!"

"Come to Me,
all who are weary and heavily burdened
[by religious rituals that provide no peace],
and I will give you rest
[refreshing your souls with salvation]."

MATTHEW 11:28 AMP

"Come to Me."

Those words of Jesus echo today, but they aren't like the words you hear when your child or someone else in your world makes that request. When your kids cry out, "Come here, Mama!" there might be an emergency at hand that requires your attention—or more likely, a mess that needs to be cleaned up or an argument that needs to be resolved. When a friend calls and says, "I'm having a tough time, could you come over?" you might feel needed and appreciated, but also that you have another responsibility to fulfill for someone you care about.

When Jesus says, "Come to Me," however, His command/request is one that is for *your* own good. It means rest, refreshment, and revitalization for your whole self: body, soul, and spirit.

You don't have to carry your burdens all alone. Jesus waits with open arms to take them off your shoulders.

He wants all of your mess and all of your stress—your exhaustion, your pain, your frustration, your sin. He wants to hear you call His name and ask Him for help, for He's always quick to come to your rescue.

Don't let one more moment go by before you go to Him. Even in the middle of your busy day, follow His instruction to "come to Me," and let Him help you every step of the way.

Lord,

I choose to obey Your call—I come to You.
Please take my burdens and help me
with all that I am facing this day.
Thank You for Your tender, loving care.

Amen.

BEAUTY IN UNEXPECTED PLACES

In everything give thanks;
for this is the will of God
in Christ Jesus for you.
I THESSALONIANS 5:18 NKJV

The day we had to move out of our family home was hard. It was the house I'd hoped to raise my kids in until they brought me grandbabies to play with—the only home they'd ever known. What was worse was the house we were moving into—I was low on finances, and I tried my best to find a suitable place, but our new landlord wasn't helpful, and the place we moved into was dirty and shabby, nothing like our beautiful house in the suburbs had been. As I sat on the floor, I put my head in my hands, realizing how much work it would take to make this place livable for me and my kids—and the disappointment overwhelmed me. But then I heard the sweet voice of my eight-year-old son say, "Look, Mommy! The sun is shining through the window on the front door! It's sooooo pretty!"

I looked up to see that he was right. He was unfazed by our circumstances and even grateful for the new door we had with a stained-glass window at the top.

I learned a valuable lesson that day. Gratitude changes

everything. Instead of moping over everything we had lost, I began to be thankful for everything I still had. We were safe, we were together, and we were going to make it, with God's help. That little light shining through the window and the sweet joy of my child's words kept a greater light shining in my heart.

Lord,

thank You for the truths that I often hear
coming from the lips of my children.
You are truly worthy of my gratitude and praise.
There is always, always something
to be thankful for!

Amen.

AN ATTITUDE OF GRATITUDE

Enter into His gates with thanksgiving,
and into His courts with praise.
Be thankful to Him, and bless His name.

PSALM 100:4 NKJV

There's so much power in an attitude of thankfulness. I know it may be hard to find anything to be thankful for in the middle of all the chaos and craziness of motherhood. When we're dealing with the tantrums and chores and laundry and dishes, it can be a challenge to remember to count our blessings. But when we take the time to appreciate what we have, even in the midst of our struggles, it can totally change our perspective. Think about it: Even when our kiddos could barely speak, we were teaching them the importance of saying "please" and "thank you." The same goes for us as grown-ups!

The apostle Paul, despite the many hardships he faced, learned to cultivate an attitude of thankfulness. Whether you are confronting a huge problem or just routine, ordinary tasks, try to be like Paul and choose to approach it with a heart full of gratitude. When you focus on all the ways in which God has blessed you, it can be like a ray of sunshine breaking through the clouds, reminding us that no matter what we are going through, God is always, ultimately, in complete control.

Whether it's a roof over your head, food on the table, or the love of your precious children, there is so much to be thankful for. God has blessed you in so many ways, Mama! Gratitude isn't just a onetime thing; it's an attitude, a way of life. Choose thankfulness over gloominess. With a heart full of gratitude, there's no telling what amazing things God has in store for you today!

Lord,

You have blessed me in so many ways—
I couldn't possibly name them all.
Thank You, thank You, thank You
for showering me with so many good things.
Your love and grace in my life is truly amazing.

Amen.

LET. IT. GO.

"For if you forgive other people
when they sin against you,
your heavenly Father will also forgive you.
But if you do not forgive others their sins,
your Father will not forgive your sins."

MATTHEW 6:14–15 NIV

Single mom life can be tough sometimes. It's probably not how you expected your life to turn out, and you may be tempted to dwell on the past. Maybe you're wondering why things turned out the way they did, why certain people treated you the way they did, or why you made certain decisions in the past.

No matter how much you ponder what happened *before*, dear mama, it's not going to change anything at all. There is no time machine; there are no do-overs in this life. What's done is done, and the best you can do is move forward. The good news is that your loving heavenly Father is right by your side, and He has a bright future planned in store for you!

Moving forward might seem easier said than done. It might feel incredibly challenging to forgive certain people, let go of certain grudges, or even forgive ourselves for the decisions we've made. But trust me: holding on to the past will only hold you back from your ultimate purpose and destiny.

And here's the kicker: Most of the time, the people who have hurt us in the past aren't sitting around thinking about it. So why should we let their actions continue to have power over us?

Choose today to let go of the past and focus on the present and the future. Be with your kids right now—do something fun and unexpected—or make a plan to do something exciting together soon. Rather than dwelling on the negativity of the past, you can make the most of what you have right now, and in the days ahead. It's time to forgive, let go, and move forward!

God,

I don't want to keep clinging
to the negativity of the past.
Help me focus on what is present today
and lift my eyes toward the bright future
You have in store for me.

Amen.

YES, YOU CAN

But one thing I do:
Forgetting what is behind and
straining toward what is ahead,
I press on toward the goal to win the prize
for which God has called me heavenward
in Christ Jesus.

PHILIPPIANS 3:13–14 NIV

God's not finished with you yet!

You woke up this morning, still breathing, still a part of this world, still your kiddos' mom, and that means that God still has a purpose for your life. Sometimes we tend to disqualify ourselves, thinking we are too damaged, too inexperienced, too young, or too old to step out in faith and pursue our dreams. But here's the thing: those are just excuses. And those excuses can hold us back from realizing our full potential and embracing the amazing plans that God has in store for us. We need to stop selling ourselves short!

God decides when our story is over—not us. And let me tell you, there is still so much hope and opportunity ahead. No matter what you've been through or where you're at right now, never place limits on what God can do through you.

If God is calling you to do something, trust me, He's fully equipped you for the task. All He asks is that you meet Him halfway. And the best part? God will give an A for effort! He's not looking for perfection; He just wants to see you stepping out in faith, believing that He can move mountains on your behalf.

Amazing things are on the horizon, my friend. With God by your side, there is nothing you can't conquer—the best is yet to come.

Lord,

my life isn't over—You've proven that by giving me breath in my lungs in this new day that has dawned. I choose to move forward today with hope, looking toward the amazing things You have in store for me. Thank You for Your grace, which fills my life.

Amen.

SLEEPING THROUGH THE STORM

Then Jesus got into the boat
and started across the lake with His disciples.
Suddenly, a fierce storm struck the lake,
with waves breaking into the boat.
But Jesus was sleeping.

MATTHEW 8:23–24

As the kids got older, I had thought things would get easier. I pondered the irony as I watched my daughter bounce out of the Jeep and head into the library for her Girl Scouts meeting. No, they weren't in diapers anymore, but the constant shuttling of my preteens to band practice, Girl Scout cookie booths, and book club was starting to wear. I had even resorted to taking a pillow to catch a quick nap in the drop-off lane at Gracie's school while we were parked.

Yes, I recognized that bone-deep weariness. It seemed like it had been there since the day the kids were born! When we are tired, everything seems just a little bit more challenging: Being patient with the kids can feel like climbing Mount Everest, and excelling at work? It's a grind to just get by many days.

Jesus gets it. He got weary from traveling too—so much

so that He fell asleep in a boat during a thunderstorm! (Which kind of makes you sleeping through your alarm seem a bit more understandable, right?) In His humanity, Jesus needed to rest and recharge, just like we do. He gets it! He gets *you*. If you are feeling deeply weary today, it's okay to ask for help—whether it's from your closest friend, a family member, or the Lord Himself. Maybe ask your boss or a colleague for a lighter load at work or ask God to help you prioritize your time better. When you're weary, pushing yourself to the brink isn't going to magically lead you to rest in the end, and the Lord understands. Take a break today and let Him handle things for a while as you get the rest you need.

Lord,

Your ability to sleep through a thunderstorm while here on the earth is truly impressive! I know the peace You experienced in the storm was a direct result of the trust relationship You have with the Father. Lord, I want to have that kind of trust in You and the Father, as well—the kind of trust that allows me to sleep in perfect peace, regardless of what storms of life threaten to rock my boat.

Amen.

SHARING THE REAL YOU

But the LORD said to Samuel,
"Don't judge by his appearance or height,
for I have rejected him. The LORD
doesn't see things the way you see them.
People judge by outward appearance,
but the LORD looks at the heart."

I SAMUEL 16:7

Let's talk about the pressure to impress, especially in our digital age of social media. It can sometimes feel like we're in a constant race to present the best versions of ourselves, right? We want our jobs, our homes, even our mothering techniques—every aspect of our lives—to look picture-perfect. But let's be real: we don't live life through an Instagram filter!

Have you recently posted something overly cheerful even when you didn't feel that way in reality? Or cropped a messy house out of a photo to make it seem like your place is cleaner than it is? It can be exhausting to keep up pretenses—and it's not doing anyone any favors. When people don't see the real you because you don't want to share the real you, everyone misses out!

How about trying something different today? Try

giving a few trusted individuals a backstage pass to the messy and clean, raw and frustrating, and joyful and jubilant parts of our lives. Letting others in on the "real deal" is the most authentic thing we can do. And you know what? Authenticity brings freedom. When we stop pretending and start being honest about the good and the bad, it's like a weight is lifted off our shoulders. Suddenly, we're not bound up by that oh-so-phony image we've been trying so hard to uphold. Instead, we are free to be ourselves—imperfections and all.

Are you keeping others locked out of some parts of your life, because they are too messy, too embarrassing, too upsetting? Take a chance and let a few people in. You'll be amazed at how much easier it becomes to share, and how much peace you'll find in being truly, unapologetically you!

God,

I know You don't look at my outward appearance or whether or not I've got it all together. You judge my heart, and You see my inner beauty. I want to lower my guard and my pretenses around others, finding true friends who love me for who I really am—the "real me." Please place these people in my life and help me to see the inner beauty in them, as well.

Amen.

LIGHT SHINES ON THE RIGHTEOUS

AND JOY
ON THE
UPRIGHT
IN HEART.

Psalm 97:11 NIV

IF YOU NEED TO RECHARGE, UNPLUG!

The Lord gives strength to His people;
the Lord blesses His people with peace.

PSALM 29:11 NIV

It's good to stay connected to other people. But these days, the temptation is often stronger to be *over*-connected than *under*-connected, isn't it? It's so easy to start scrolling on social media and lose track of time. Most of our interest is beneficial: We want to know what our kids are up to in their classrooms or what's happening in the PTA, stay in the loop with our friends, and keep tabs on the latest news that's taking place in our communities and in the world. And thanks to today's technology, it's all right at our fingertips.

If we aren't careful, however, staying overly connected can turn into an obsession. Do you ever feel a pang of panic when you realize you left the house without your phone? Or do you find yourself mindlessly scrolling through your social media feeds for far too long instead of just going to sleep? It happens to the best of us. It's easy to get caught in the FOMO (fear of missing out) trap!

But just like we teach our kids about balance in life—whether it's with their screen time or what snacks they eat—we need to practice what we preach. Sometimes we need to unplug to truly recharge.

Try turning off your phone for a little while, maybe set aside the screens for an evening, and just be present in the moment. Hug your kiddos tight, feel the breeze on your face, and let yourself laugh at something silly. When you take even a short time to unplug, the benefits are so worth it. You'll find a rest that refreshes not just your body, but your mind and your spirit too. And who knows? You might just discover a whole new appreciation for being present in the here and now, the beauty of this very moment.

Lord,

there is so much going on in my life at times that I can barely keep up. This fast-paced world has me running ragged most days—and a lot of the problem, truthfully, comes from my electronic devices. Calls, texts, social media, email—sometimes I just need to let it all go for a bit and focus on You. Help me to keep my priorities straight as I commit to unplug the best I can and recharge my spirit in Your presence.

Amen.

REACH OUT TO HIM

Morning, noon, and night
I cry out in my distress,
and the Lord hears my voice.
PSALM 55:17

In this journey through life, we often encounter challenges that test our strength and resilience. For me, one of the worst has been dealing with chronic pain. This kind of physical pain is a harsh reality that many of us grapple with daily, whether it's from battling migraines or facing the complexities of autoimmune diseases, the burden of pain can weigh heavily on our hearts and our bodies.

But even in the middle of suffering, we can find comfort in what we learn from God's Word. In fact, the book of Luke recounts the story of a woman who likely endured chronic pain: She had dealt with twelve long years of bleeding in her body, likely leaving her anemic, weak, and in pain. She sought help from many doctors during that time but found no relief. And despite countless attempts by others to heal her, she found no remedy until she encountered Jesus.

In a crowd teeming with desperation, this woman dared to believe in the transformative power of faith. And with a simple touch of Jesus' garment, she was instantaneously healed. While not all of our own prayers are answered with such immediacy, when we reach out to Jesus in faith ourselves, we, too, will find the relief we need. He is intimately acquainted with our pain and suffering, and He longs to help!

Beyond that, your journey, even in pain, has a purpose beyond what meets the eye. Through your own experiences, you—and likely your kiddos too—will gain a profound sense of empathy for other people enduring similar trials. Your resilience in the face of adversity can serve as a beacon of hope for those who feel overwhelmed by the pain.

As you reach out to the Lord, know that He hears you, and He offers a promise of healing and restoration. Your pain does not define you, Mama! Your journey is a testimony of your strength and resilience—to your kids and to all those around you.

Lord,

I reach out to You right now.
Heal me. Restore my life.
Bring me into the light of Your love and
show Yourself strong in my life.

Amen.

PLEASING GOD, NOT PEOPLE

Obviously, I'm not trying to win
the approval of people, but of God.
If pleasing people were my goal,
I would not be Christ's servant.
GALATIANS 1:10

Have you ever experienced that sinking feeling when someone tells you they're "disappointed" in you? It's like a punch in the gut, isn't it? Hearing those words from parents, teachers, or coaches is never easy. Some of us—ahem, ME—have a natural inclination to bend over backward to keep everyone happy, but let's face it: trying to please everyone is like trying to catch water in a sieve—exhausting and ultimately futile.

Here's the thing: You can't be all things to all people. It's just not humanly possible. So, instead of running yourself ragged trying to meet everyone else's expectations, maybe it's time to set some new priorities and better boundaries. You can still say yes to *some* things, but you shouldn't feel *obligated* to say yes to *everything*. Sometimes the most powerful word in your vocabulary is a simple, but firm "no." Remember, putting God first and taking care of your own well-being are essential steps in finding balance in the middle of life's demands.

So, are you feeling the need to hit the *pause* button on people-pleasing? It's okay to take a step back and reassess what's going on. Ask God to guide you as you prioritize His will above all else. Seek His wisdom and strength to set healthy boundaries that protect your time, energy, and peace of mind. When you learn to say no to the demands of others and yes to God's plan for your life, you'll discover a newfound sense of freedom and fulfillment. And that's so worth it!

So, dear mama, take heart. You don't have to carry the weight of the world on your shoulders. Trust in God's guidance, and don't be afraid to occasionally put yourself first (GASP!)—at least when necessary. By honoring your own human needs and aligning your priorities with God's will, you'll find the balance and peace you've been seeking.

Lord,

the desire to please other people can be strong sometimes. I want to set healthy boundaries with those around me and seek to please You first. I know that when I do, You will bring peace and balance to my life.

Amen.

DON'T BE A WORRYWART!

He personally carried our sins
in His body on the cross
so that we can be dead to sin
and live for what is right.
By His wounds you are healed.

I PETER 2:24

"Don't be a worrywart!" Did your mom ever tell you those words when something was causing you to fret as a kid—or even now, as an adult? Maybe it's just a "Southern thing," but they are words to live by!

Life sure has a way of piling on the worries, doesn't it? From everyday stresses to deep-seated fears, it's easy to feel overwhelmed by the weight of our burdens. Maybe you're wrestling with sin, awaiting test results, or worried about a kiddo who is struggling in math. Perhaps you're feeling the strain of single parenthood, of seemingly "going it alone," struggling with feelings of loneliness and inadequacy. Whatever challenges you're facing, know this: you don't have to bear them alone.

What is weighing on your heart and mind today? Whether it's the health of your pet, the demands of work, financial worries, or family struggles, commit to bringing it to the Lord. In your mind's eye, envision yourself laying each burden at the foot of the cross.

Why do we come to the cross? Because that's where Jesus invites us to bring our burdens—and then leave them there. He doesn't want us to carry the weight of our worries; He wants to shoulder them for us. When we surrender our fears, our shame, our anxieties, and our doubts to Him, He offers us His peace and His rest in return.

So, release your grip on those burdens today. Trust that Jesus is ready and willing to take them from you. Allow His love and grace to wash over you, filling you with the assurance that you are not alone in your struggles. As you leave your cares at the cross, embrace the freedom and the peace that come from entrusting your life into His hands.

Remember, dear mama, there is nothing too heavy for Jesus to bear. He conquered the cross—for you and for me—and He is willing to help you right now.

Lord,

I'd rather trust in You than be a worrywart today.
I lay my burdens and concerns at Your feet.
I know You can handle them. Help me
to remember that You are fully in control.
I turn my worries over to You.

Amen.

THE MAKER OF THE TREES

"Wherever your treasure is, there the desires of your heart will also be."

MATTHEW 6:21

Wouldn't it be a breeze if money grew on trees? You could just pluck a bill whenever you needed it, and off you would go! But, sadly, life doesn't work like that. Yet, maybe it's for the best. Imagine if we had everything we wanted at our fingertips; we might never learn to lean on the Lord!

Isn't it fascinating how those with the least material possessions often trust God the most? It's pretty easy to understand; they've witnessed His provision firsthand. When we rely solely on ourselves, we risk forgetting the true Source of our blessings. Instead of seeing our own efforts as the provider of everything we need, let's recognize God as the ultimate Provider.

While we may not have a money tree, we've been blessed with something even better: a relationship with the Creator of all things. Through Christ, we have access to the One who *actually made the trees*—and everything else we see in our world. Why wouldn't He be willing and able to provide for us—whether it's food, money, support, help, or anything else? So let's rest in this truth and trust God to meet our every need.

Remember, dear mama, even when finances seem tight, God's abundance is limitless. He's got your back!

Dear heavenly Father,

when I look around me, I am reminded of all
that You have made and how powerful You are.
I don't need money to grow on trees
to have my needs met—I only need to trust in You,
the Maker of the trees. Thank You for
taking care of me and mine.

Amen.

A SEASON FOR ALL THINGS

And after you have suffered a little while, the God of all grace, who has called you to his eternal glory in Christ, will himself restore, confirm, strengthen, and establish you.

I PETER 5:10 ESV

Lazy days of summer come to a close, and the weather turns cooler. Once school starts, it seems the holidays are approaching in the blink of an eye. Then cold weather and the new year; then spring break is here—and gone in a flash. And soon, it's summer all over again. The kids are a year older, and we start the cycle again.

Just as the earth turns and cycles through the seasons of the natural world, so, too, do we move in the ebb and flow of the different seasons and stages—in our own lives and in the lives of our kids, our families, and our friends.

Life is full of these kinds of seasons, isn't it? Some of them pass by in a flash, like those chaotic teenage years, while others seem to stretch on endlessly, like the sleepless nights you spend with a newborn. Maybe right now, you find yourself in a season that you didn't quite anticipate—one filled with loss and pain. You can rest assured, though, another season will come—one filled with joy and hope.

As moms, we often find ourselves looking ahead—to the next milestone, the next challenge, the next phase of life. If you're in a tough season right now, you might be eagerly awaiting relief, hoping for brighter days ahead. But sometimes God asks us to stay put, to weather the storms for a little while longer. In those moments, it can feel downright exhausting. But take heart, dear mama, because relief is on the horizon.

You see, even when we don't quite understand it, God's plan is always at work. There's a purpose for every season, every trial, every moment of joy and sorrow. So take a deep breath and rest in the knowledge that the Lord is right there beside you, guiding you every step of the way. He's whispering to your heart, "I've got this. You can trust Me."

So whatever season you find yourself in today, know that it's all a part of God's perfect plan. Trust in Him, lean on Him, and find your rest in His unwavering love.

Winter, spring, summer, fall—

You, O Lord, have made them all. Thank You for the seasons You bring forth in Your beautiful world. And thank You, too, for the beautiful seasons in my life. As I watch my children grow and learn, I see Your purposes unfolding in our lives—and it's an amazing thing!

Amen.

THE RUNNING OF MY WORLD

For a child has been born—
for us! The gift of a son—for us!
He'll take over the running of the world.
His names will be: Amazing Counselor,
Strong God, Eternal Father, Prince of Wholeness.

ISAIAH 9:6 THE MESSAGE

Dear mama, have you ever had one of those nights when you had a million things to do, but instead, you ended up snoozing on the couch? I've been there too. And when you wake up to an even longer to-do list, it can feel like the weight of the world is on your shoulders.

As a single mom, it often seems like everything falls right onto you. You're not just providing for your kids' physical needs; you're also creating a home where they feel safe, loved, and supported. But in the midst of all the busyness, don't forget to take care of yourself too.

Friend, be kind to yourself. If you're feeling weary, it's okay to hit the pause button and rest. And if it feels like you're constantly playing catch-up, maybe it's time to ease up on those expectations you've set for yourself.

The prophet Isaiah foretold a Savior who would come and "take over the running of the world." While we have no control over when that will eventually happen, what we *can* control is the running of our own worlds—our households, our families, and all that that entails. Wouldn't it be nice to turn that over to the One the prophet calls "Amazing Counselor," "Strong God," "Eternal Father," and "Prince of Wholeness"?

In His lifetime here on earth, Jesus invited the weary and burdened to come to Him. He didn't scold them for falling behind or lecture them about their to-do lists. No, He welcomed them with open arms and promised to carry their burdens. He offers the same to you this day—so why not take Him up on that offer?

Instead of listening to the negative voices in your head, tune in to the words of love and grace that Jesus has for you. Let His peace wash over you, soothing your tired soul and giving you the rest you so desperately need. Take a deep breath, dear mama, and let go of those heavy burdens. Jesus is here to carry them for you.

Precious Savior,

You are the King of kings and the Lord of lords. You are more than capable of running my world—and I commit today to allowing You to do just that. I hand my burdens to You. Thank You for Your peace that passes all understanding.

Amen.

THIS VERY MOMENT

Teach us to number our days,
that we may gain a heart of wisdom.
PSALM 90:12 NIV

Most moms have heard the saying, "The days are long, but the years are short"—and we sure do feel it! It's something we moms know all too well. It's easy to lose sight of the present moment in the reaching forward to the next step, the next stage, the next item on our list of to-dos. How often do you catch yourself thinking about what's coming next? Maybe you're counting down the minutes until bedtime or eagerly awaiting the weekend or dreaming about what the future holds. But in the midst of all that anticipation, don't overlook the beauty of the present moment.

Here's the thing: Right now, in this very moment, God is showering you with His blessings. He's giving you the gift of breath, the rhythm of your heartbeat, and the warmth of the morning sun. Every laugh from your child, every act of kindness from a stranger, every vibrant sunset is a reminder of His love and presence in your life. And guess what? This day, this hour, this minute, it's a gift from God too, tailor-made just for you.

So why rush through it? Instead of constantly looking ahead to the next thing coming up, take a moment to pause and soak in the beauty of the here and now. Whether it's the simple joy of sharing a meal with your kids, the peaceful quiet of an early morning, or the sense of accomplishment after a long day's work, there's so much to be grateful for in this present moment.

Don't let the busyness of life steal your joy. Open your eyes to the blessings that surround you and let yourself rest in the joy of the present. After all, tomorrow will come soon enough—but today is a gift meant to be cherished!

Father,

this very minute, I realize, is a gift from You.
I'm slowing down now to savor the joys it brings—
the sound of my children's laughter,
the warm sun on my face, the "good" tired
after a day's worth of productive work.
You bring so many blessings—too many to count.
Thank You for Your goodness in my life.

Amen.

HONEST FORGIVENESS

We know how much God loves us,
and we have put our trust in His love.
God is love, and all who live in love
live in God, and God lives in them.

I JOHN 4:16

Going through a divorce, by its very definition, results in hurts and offenses that are nearly unavoidable. The breaking apart of a family is an extremely painful process for everyone involved. So, it's obvious that some level of forgiveness will be needed between ex-spouses. What surprised me more during my divorce, though, were the offenses and anger that came from other people outside of our family. Friends and people from church took sides, with gossip flying and resentment festering. In many ways, those hurts and offenses were far more challenging for me to forgive, simply because they were so unexpected.

Have you been hurt by someone close to you? Maybe it was a harsh word spoken in anger, a betrayal of trust, or a painful experience that still lingers in your heart. Whatever the source of your pain, holding on to bitterness, resentment, or a desire for revenge can weigh you down and keep you from experiencing true freedom and peace.

But here's the good news: you don't have to carry that

burden alone. In I John 4:16, we're reminded that God calls us to live in love, even in the face of hurt and betrayal. It's not always easy, but it's possible—with God's help.

Take a moment to ask yourself: *What hurts am I holding on to? What wounds do I need to let go of in order to experience the fullness of God's love and peace?* Then, invite Jesus into those places of pain and brokenness, and ask Him to help you release them into His care.

Remember, healing takes time. It's okay if you don't feel better overnight. Just keep turning to Jesus, day by day, and trust that He is at work in your heart, replacing your pain with His love, joy, peace, kindness, and hope.

As you go about your day today, know that you are not alone. Jesus sees your pain and longs to heal your heart and help you love again. Trust in His unfailing love and let go of those hurts that are weighing you down. As you do, you'll find the freedom and peace that only He can give.

Heavenly Father,

someone has hurt me deeply, and my heart is wounded. Please pour Your healing balm over my injured feelings, over the deep pain in my soul. I choose to forgive the person who hurt me, but I need Your help. Thank You for Your perfect love and the peace and freedom You offer me today.

Amen.

MONEY MATTERS

"Look at the ravens. They don't plant or harvest or store food in barns, for God feeds them. And you are far more valuable to Him than any birds!"

LUKE 12:24

When I was just three years old, I sang a duet in church with my mom on Mother's Day. It's a cherished memory we both still share. You may have heard of the song we chose: "His Eye Is on the Sparrow." Its lyrics speak of how the Lord so faithfully watches over the little sparrows and lovingly cares for their needs, but the final line shares what's most important: "I know He's watching me."

Mama, do you ever feel lost and alone, even uncared for, while unpaid bills just keep piling up and you can't stretch your paycheck far enough? From unexpected expenses to the everyday costs of raising kids, it's easy to feel overwhelmed by financial worries. But you don't have to carry that burden all by yourself.

Take this moment to breathe and remember that you serve a God who cares about every detail of your life, including your finances. He sees your needs and promises to provide for you, no matter how dire the situation may seem. He loves you just as He loves the birds and other creatures He constantly cares for—and He longs to meet your every need.

So, today, I want to encourage you to take your worries to the Lord. Whether it's a looming repair bill, concerns about your job security, or simply feeling like there's just never enough to go around, lay it all at His feet. He's not just the God of the big miracles; He's also the God of the everyday provision.

As you entrust your finances to Him, remember to also take practical steps to manage your money wisely. Create a budget, look for ways to save, and seek out resources and support in your community. God often works through ordinary means to meet our needs, so don't hesitate to reach out for help when you need it.

Above all, hold on to the promise that God is faithful. He's been faithful in the past, and He'll be faithful again. So, even when the hits to your bank account seem to come all at once, trust that He's working behind the scenes to provide for you and your family.

Today, choose to release your financial worries and trust in God's provision. He's got you in the palm of His hand, and He'll never let you down.

Lord,

You are so faithful to provide everything I need. I know that Your eye is on the sparrow, as it is on all Your beloved creatures. Thank You for also watching over me.

Amen.

MAY
THE LORD
OF PEACE
HIMSELF
GIVE YOU
PEACE

AT ALL
TIMES
AND
IN EVERY
WAY.

II Thessalonians 3:16
NIV

LISTEN TO YOUR BODY

Let all that I am praise the Lord;
may I never forget the good things He does for me.
He forgives all my sins and heals all my diseases.
He redeems me from death and
crowns me with love and tender mercies.
PSALM 103:2–4

Oh no. I could feel it coming on. My son had been dealing with a cold and sinus infection he'd brought home from the "petri dish" of elementary school. And now, the thing I had greatly feared had now come upon me.

The scratchy throat.

The achy muscles in my body.

The utter fatigue, pulling me to the ground.

My body was sending up flares, warning me that exhaustion was on the horizon, and I knew I was going to have to set aside some time to rest and get well.

Just like when you're getting sick, your body has ways of letting you know when you're pushing yourself too hard. Maybe you're feeling constantly drained, or the thought of how much you have to get done in the next week fills you with dread. Whatever the signs may be, it's important to listen to what your body is telling you.

Give yourself permission to slow down and rest. Take a

sick day from work or ask for help with that overwhelming project. Lean on your support system—whether it's a coworker to help you out in the office, your oldest child to help you with chores around the house, or even a pizza delivery guy to bring you dinner!

Your well-being is important, and sometimes that means putting your own needs first. Remember, it's *not* selfish to take care of yourself; it's *necessary* for your health and happiness.

So, if your body is telling you to rest, don't ignore it. If you feel a cold coming on, take a sick day and fend it off. Embrace any unexpected opportunity to recharge and rejuvenate. Your body will thank you, and you'll be better equipped to tackle whatever challenges come your way.

Today, let's prioritize self-care and listen to the messages our bodies are sending us. Because when we take care of ourselves, we're better able to take care of those we love.

Lord,

You know what is best for the people You've created—
in their body, soul, and spirit. Today I commit to
resting and taking care of my body. Help me to stay
strong—in every way—so I can continue to care
for the children You've entrusted to my care.

Amen.

"O NORMAL DAY!"

On a good day, enjoy yourself;
on a bad day, examine your conscience.
God arranges for both kinds of days
so that we won't take anything for granted.

ECCLESIASTES 7:14 THE MESSAGE

There's a saying by Mary Jean Irion that I've really appreciated through my single-mom journey: "Normal day, let me be aware of the treasure you are." Those days when there are no crises, no crazy expectations, no super highs or super lows—that's where life is really lived. It's a wonderful place, really—just living a "normal" day with your kids, whatever "normal" might look like for you.

Take a moment to reflect on the journey you've been on—the highs, the lows, and everything in between. You may find unexpected pain and grief tucked between moments of joy and blessings. But through it all, you'll see that each day unfolded just as it should have.

As you look ahead, remember that you can trust all your tomorrows to God. But today? Today is your opportunity to fully embrace the present moment. It's where hope comes alive, where blessings abound, and where you'll find the strength you need to face whatever comes your way.

Jesus reminded us that each day has its own share of troubles. So, instead of worrying about tomorrow, focus on making the most of today. From the gentle light of dawn to the vibrant hues of sunset, there's plenty of time to fill with work, pleasure, cares, and dreams.

So don't rush through today, trying to make time move faster. Instead, savor each moment as it unfolds. Embrace the beauty of the here and now, and trust that God has a plan for every step of your journey. Today is a gift, filled with endless possibilities for you, your kids, and the Lord to explore together.

Lord,

thank You so much for the "normal" days
that come between the highs and the lows—
where life is truly lived.
I cherish every moment in this amazing life
You've blessed me with.
You are so good to me.

Amen.

CLOTHED WITH COMPASSION

Therefore, as God's chosen people,
holy and dearly loved,
clothe yourselves with compassion,
kindness, humility,
gentleness and patience.
COLOSSIANS 3:12 NIV

Have you ever noticed how laughter and smiles have an amazing power to transform even the grouchiest of faces? When you see someone feeling down, your natural instinct might be to reach out with a funny story or some cheerful words to lift their spirits. This is a beautiful act of compassion—one that might feel a bit rare in today's world.

In a culture where people often feel cautious or hesitant to extend kindness to strangers, being compassionate can sometimes feel like taking a chance. But let me tell you, those moments of compassion can make all the difference in someone's life.

Think about the times when you've sent a card or flowers to a friend in need, or offered up a prayer when someone you love was hurting. That's compassion in action. And I bet you've experienced the warmth of compassion yourself when others have reached out to support you during tough times.

Compassionate people are like little reminders of God's love for us. They ease the pain of those who are suffering and offer a glimmer of hope in the midst of darkness. They show us that we're not alone, that we're deeply cared for, and that there's still kindness and goodness in the world.

So, let's embrace our calling to be compassionate, even when it feels like a risk. Because when we choose compassion, we're not just spreading kindness—we're sharing God's love with those who need it the most.

Lord,

thank You for the compassion You've shown me,
for the tender mercies I've received from Your hand.
Show me the ones around me who need
a compassionate touch and help me to share
Your love with them in meaningful ways.

Amen.

THE ULTIMATE FRIEND

"I no longer call you servants, because a servant does not know his master's business. Instead, I have called you friends, for everything that I learned from My Father I have made known to you."

JOHN 15:15 NIV

Friends who just "get you" are one of life's greatest blessings. You know those friends—even if you haven't seen each other in ages, it feels like no time has passed at all. There's no need for small talk or awkwardness—just pure comfort and connection, like a warm hug just being around them.

Jesus is the ultimate Friend, and He's just like that. He knows every part of you—the good, the bad, and the messy in-betweens—and He loves you unconditionally. Think about it: He sees you at your best and your worst, and yet His love for you never wavers. It's a love that's deeper and more steadfast than any other.

Even if it's been a while since you last talked to Jesus, know that He's always there, ready to welcome you back with open arms. Imagine Him running toward you, eager to embrace you and remind you of His unwavering faithfulness. In His friendship, you'll find the rest and comfort your soul craves.

It's a lot like how you feel about your own children: Jesus' love for you is unending and unconditional. He's the Friend who understands you like no other, and His presence brings a sense of peace and reassurance to your weary heart.

Take a moment today to reconnect with your most perfect Friend. Whether it's through prayer, reading His Word, or simply sitting in His presence, lean into the comfort and joy that His friendship offers.

Dearest Jesus,

You are the best Friend I will ever have.
You are always there to listen,
to help, to support, and to comfort.
Help me to share Your love and friendship with others
and teach my children to trust in You
as their best Friend too.

Amen.

RUN THE RACE

Forgetting what is behind and straining toward what is ahead, I press on toward the goal to win the prize for which God has called me heavenward in Christ Jesus.

PHILIPPIANS 3:13–14 NIV

Back when I was in college, I used to love to run. The Christian university I attended required every student to run three miles every semester, as it valued the ideal of keeping the physical body as strong as the mind, but that wasn't why I ran as much as I did. I loved the release from stress it brought me, along with those good endorphins that helped me stay awake to study the rest of the night.

It's great to get out there and exercise; nothing can clear your mind and reset your thoughts like a good workout, including a jog.

What about you? Do you love to run, or do you hate it? Running is one of those activities that can push us to our limits, especially when it feels like every step is a struggle. But you know what? That perseverance, that determination to keep going even when it's tough—that's what makes us stronger.

Paul knew a thing or two about perseverance. In Philippians 3, he compared his spiritual journey to a footrace, with Jesus being the ultimate prize. Paul didn't have it all figured out, but he was determined to keep pressing forward, leaving behind the mistakes and regrets of the past. His goal was clear: to know Jesus more deeply and to one day reach heaven to gain the prize of being with his Savior for eternity.

What "race" are you running right now in life? Maybe it's something big, like furthering your education or advancing in your career. Or maybe it's something more personal, like breaking free from old habits or overcoming past mistakes.

Isaiah 43:18 reminds us to let go of the past and focus on what's ahead. It's easy to get bogged down by our past failures or regrets, but dwelling on them only holds us back from reaching our full potential. Instead, let's fix our eyes on Jesus and the future, knowing that God has great things in store for us.

Keep pressing forward, dear mama. Even on the days when it feels like you're running uphill, remember that every step forward brings you closer to your goals. And know that with God by your side, there's nothing you can't overcome.

Father,

I'm letting go of the past and pressing forward in You. I fix my eyes on Jesus as I continue in the race You've set before me.

Amen.

BETRAYED WITH A KISS

But Jesus asked him,
"Judas, are you betraying the Son of Man with a kiss?"
LUKE 22:48 NIV

Betrayal causes a very deep wound. When someone you trusted lets you down, it can feel like your whole world is falling apart. The pain cuts deep, and it takes time to heal.

Think about Jesus and Judas. Judas, one of Jesus' closest friends, betrayed Him with a kiss—a sign of affection twisted into an act of deception. It must have been heartbreaking for Jesus to see someone He cared about turn against Him. But even in the face of betrayal, Jesus didn't lose hope.

After His death and resurrection, Jesus appeared to His disciples, offering them new life and new hope. Despite Judas' betrayal, Jesus' message of hope changed the world—and it continues to impact us today. That same hope can bring healing to our own hurts and wounds.

So how do we move forward from betrayal? It starts with forgiveness. Forgiving someone who has hurt us isn't easy, but it's essential for our own healing. When we choose to forgive, we release the power that betrayal holds over us and open ourselves up to God's healing grace.

But forgiveness doesn't mean forgetting or pretending like the betrayal never happened. It's about acknowledging the pain and choosing to let go of the bitterness and resentment that can hold us back.

Instead, let's hold on to hope. Hope that God can bring beauty from ashes, that He can turn our pain into something beautiful. And let's allow that hope to undergird our relationships, knowing that even when people let us down, God's love remains steadfast and true.

So, if you're struggling with betrayal today, know that you're not alone. Lean on God's strength and allow His hope to guide you through the healing process.

Dear Jesus,

a kiss is such a personal, intimate gesture, but that is how Judas chose to betray You while You were here on the earth. So I know You get it—You know how I feel. But You also cause me to move past the betrayal I've experienced and into a brighter tomorrow with You. Heal my heart this day and fill me with Your hope and peace as I choose to walk in forgiveness toward everyone.

Amen.

EVERYTHING. YES, *EVERYTHING*!

And we know that God causes everything to work together for the good of those who love God and are called according to His purpose for them.

ROMANS 8:28

The Bible tells us that God causes everything to work together for our good. How much is *everything*? That means all of it! Divorce? That's included. Broken-down relationships? Yep, that too. Too much month at the end of your money? That just helps you learn to trust God more!

Have you ever felt like you've hit a dead end, like you've exhausted all your options and there's nowhere left to turn? It's a tough spot to be in, especially when you're trying to build a better life for yourself and your kids. Believe me, I get it.

But you're not out of possibilities—not even close. God has a way of turning our most challenging situations into opportunities for growth and transformation. Even when it feels like you're stuck in a waiting period, God is at work behind the scenes, orchestrating His perfect plan for your life.

Every difficulty you face has a purpose. It may not be

immediately clear, but God is using it to shape you and prepare you for what lies ahead. So instead of seeing this waiting period as a waste, try to view it as an opportunity for God to work in your life in ways you never imagined.

Here's the good news: God's plan for you is far greater than anything you could ever dream up on your own. So even when things don't happen as quickly or as smoothly as you hoped, trust that God is working all things together for your good.

Think of it like this: God is the ultimate designer, and He's creating a masterpiece with your life. Every twist and turn, every delay and detour, is just another brushstroke in His grand design. So keep trusting, keep believing, and keep moving forward with faith.

And remember, you're not alone in this journey. God is with you every step of the way, guiding you, encouraging you, and cheering you on. So hold on to hope, dear mama, and trust that the best is yet to come.

Father,

there is purpose in my pain.
I am trusting You to bring good things from all
the "everythings" I am going through today.
Thank You for always keeping Your promises.

Amen.

REST FOR YOUR SOUL

Truly my soul finds rest in God;
my salvation comes from Him.
Yes, my soul, find rest in God;
my hope comes from Him.

PSALM 62:1,5 NIV

Have you been burning the midnight oil, pushing through exhaustion to tackle your never-ending to-do list? It's a scenario most single moms can relate to—feeling like there's always something else demanding our attention, even when our bodies are begging for rest.

Here's a gentle reminder: not everything has to be done right this second. Sure, some tasks are nonnegotiable, but others can wait until tomorrow—or even later than that. It's all about prioritizing and recognizing what truly needs your immediate attention.

The next time you're feeling overwhelmed, take a moment to ask yourself: Is there a real consequence if I don't finish this today? Sometimes pressing on is necessary, but other times, it's just our own pride or stubbornness that keeps us from hitting the pause button.

It's easy to fall into the trap of thinking that everything is urgent and that the weight of the world rests solely on our shoulders. The truth is that it's okay to let go of perfectionism and allow ourselves the grace to rest, even if it means leaving a few things undone.

So if the dishes are piled in the sink or the laundry remains unfolded, give yourself permission to step back and prioritize your self-care. Remember, a rested mind and body are far more valuable than a checked-off to-do list.

And here's the beautiful part: when we prioritize rest, we actually become more effective and efficient in the long run. So take a deep breath, dear mama, and let go of the pressure to do it all. Embrace rest, knowing that tomorrow is another day to pick up where you left off.

Lord,

I'm so tired. Help me to let go
of unimportant tasks today and get some rest.
The dishes will still be there tomorrow;
I choose to spend quiet time
in Your peaceful presence today.

Amen.

ENJOY THE LITTLE THINGS

The heavens declare the glory of God;
the skies proclaim the work of His hands.
PSALM 19:1 NIV

Have you ever noticed how children have this incredible ability to find joy in the smallest of things? A bubble bath in Mom's Jacuzzi tub, a flower or a puppy or a swing in the park ... Kids can spot wonder and delight where adults often overlook it. It's as if they have a special lens that allows them to appreciate the magic in every moment.

Somewhere along the way, many of us lost that childlike sense of wonder. Life's responsibilities, especially as single mothers, can weigh heavy on our shoulders, leaving little room for spontaneity or awe. We're so caught up in the busyness of survival mode that we forget to pause and truly experience the beauty around us.

Today I encourage you to slow down and embrace the simple joys that surround you. Take a moment to watch the sunrise, relish each bite of a delicious meal, or marvel at the intricacies of nature. These small but precious moments are gifts from a loving Creator, waiting for us to notice and appreciate them.

So, give yourself permission to step off the treadmill

of constant busyness. Allow yourself to be present in the here and now, fully immersed in the beauty of everyday life. As you do, you'll discover that even in the middle of life's challenges, there is still so much wonder and joy to be found.

Let's reclaim that childlike wonder and curiosity, embracing each moment with open hearts and grateful spirits. After all, life is too short to rush past all the beauty that surrounds us.

God,

You have created such a marvelous world for us to experience. Let me not get so busy that I lose my appreciation for the beauty that surrounds me. Help me to cultivate an attitude of childlike joy and wonder at all the amazing things You bring my way.

Amen.

DREAM BIG

"My sheep hear My voice,
and I know them, and they follow Me."
JOHN 10:27 NKJV

Have you ever felt like your dreams were just too far out of reach because of your role as a single mom? Maybe you've hesitated to even entertain the idea of dreaming big because you were afraid of what might happen if you dared to hope. If that's the case, dear mama, it's time to shift your perspective.

God has a way of speaking to us in various ways—through His Word; through that still, small voice within us; through the circumstances we face; and even through the people He places in our lives. He's constantly guiding us, nudging us toward His will and purpose for our lives. But in order to hear His voice, we need to tune in and listen closely.

Learning to recognize God's voice in the middle of the noise of life is key. It's about cultivating that sensitivity to His leading, allowing His Spirit to speak to our hearts and direct our steps. Sometimes He may be gently urging us to revisit those dreams we've tucked away, encouraging us to breathe new life into them. Other times, He may be guiding us to dream even bigger than before.

Take a moment now to quiet your mind and reflect on those dreams that once filled your heart with excitement. Don't let fear or doubt hold you back any longer. Instead, trust in God's leading and take those small steps forward, one at a time. As you follow His guidance and dare to dream again, remember that He is the One who has planted those desires within you. And when you align your dreams with His purpose, there's no limit to what you can achieve.

Go ahead—embrace those dreams, no matter how big or small they may seem. With God by your side, the possibilities are endless.

Lord,

thank You for the dreams You have placed in my heart.
I will continue to follow You as You lead me
into the bright future You have prepared just for me.

Amen.

THOSE WHO LIVE IN THE SHELTER OF THE MOST HIGH

WILL FIND REST IN THE SHADOW OF THE ALMIGHTY.

Psalm 91:1

NEW LIFE AHEAD

"I have told you all this
so that you may have peace in Me.
Here on earth you will have
many trials and sorrow. But take heart,
because I have overcome the world."

JOHN 16:33

Have you ever felt like you were hiding away from the challenges and pains of life, much like a caterpillar in its cocoon? Maybe you've found yourself retreating, building walls around your heart in an attempt to shield yourself from the difficulties you face. But what if I told you that there's beauty waiting to emerge from within?

Just like the caterpillar transforms into a butterfly within its cocoon, you, too, have the power to undergo a transformation—a renewal of hope and strength that prepares you to rise above life's challenges. Jesus Himself acknowledged that troubles are inevitable in this world, but He also promised us hope. He assured us that He has overcome the world, and His Spirit dwells within us, empowering us to overcome any obstacle we may encounter.

Remaining hidden away in our cocoons is not the end of the journey. Eventually, we must emerge and face the world anew. But when we do, we have the opportunity to see things from a fresh perspective, to view the world with renewed eyes. Even in our darkest moments of rest and reflection, we can find the courage to strengthen our wings and embrace the transformation that hope brings.

So, dear friend, take heart in knowing that the process of transformation is already underway. Allow hope to take root deep within your heart and soul, guiding you as you spread your wings and take flight into a future filled with promise and possibility.

With faith as your guide and hope as your companion, there's no limit to the heights you can reach.

Lord,

I'm coming out of my cocoon!
Thank You for transforming my life
in so many beautiful and unexpected ways.
I place my hope in You.

Amen.

WHAT NO THIEF CAN STEAL

"The thief's purpose is
to steal and kill and destroy.
My purpose is to give them
a rich and satisfying life."

JOHN 10:10

Moving day had come and gone. It had already been challenging and depressing in the most emotional of ways—leaving our beautiful home and moving into the only place I could afford at the time: a run-down, dirty older house that, frankly, had seen better days. Adding insult to injury, it soon became obvious that during the course of our move, someone had stolen several of our electronic devices, including my kids' cherished Xbox and several favorite games.

It's not just in our personal struggles that we feel the sting of being robbed. Since the dawn of time, Satan has been at work, stealing our joy, extinguishing our hope, and tearing apart our relationships with God and others. Yet, in the midst of this darkness, the light of the cross shines brightly.

Despite Satan's relentless attempts to wreak havoc in our lives, he cannot lay claim to our true life—the life we have in Christ, hidden safely with Him. While the enemy may delight in disrupting our circumstances and throwing our lives into chaos, God is faithful to restore what has been lost—and He can stop the thief right in his tracks. In His hands, our brokenness becomes a canvas for His redemption, and He brings healing and wholeness in unexpected and miraculous ways.

Dear mama, take heart in knowing that you are not alone in your struggle. Though the road may be difficult, God is with you every step of the way. His love is unchanging, His promises are true, and His faithfulness endures forever.

My family eventually replaced the stolen Xbox with a newer, better version, but we also learned what was truly most important: our trust in the Lord and our love for each other.

Lord,

You are so faithful to restore what the enemy has stolen from my life. But even more important than the restoration of material things is the renewal of my hope and trust in Your goodness and love.

Amen.

NEVER ALONE

God is our refuge and strength,
an ever-present help in trouble. . . .
The Lord Almighty is with us;
the God of Jacob is our fortress.

PSALM 46:1, 7 NIV

Sick kids. Unpaid bills. Too many things to remember and keep track of. It's hard carrying the weight of all this alone—especially when it is something that seems to be serious, like the cough that could be "more than a cold" in my asthmatic son or the rattling in the Jeep's engine that I can still hear, no matter how loudly I turn up the radio.

There are days when walking the path alone seems to amplify the challenges we already face as single mothers. While we may be surrounded by caring friends and family members, no one truly understands the weight of our responsibilities like we do. The fears, the decisions looming on the horizon—they can bear down on us at times with an intensity that's hard to shake.

In the middle of all of this, Psalm 46 speaks to our troubled hearts, reminding us we are not alone: "God is our refuge and strength, an ever-present help in trouble" (v. 1). Even when life throws the unexpected our way, God remains our steadfast support in this very moment.

Penned by an unknown author and sung in ancient worship, Psalm 46 celebrates the sovereign care of the Lord Almighty. It doesn't promise immunity from hardship; rather, it assures us that our true essence—our very core—is safeguarded by His unfailing love. Just as Jerusalem found security in God's dwelling place, we, too, can trust in His presence within us, through His Spirit (vv. 4–5). Regardless of what each new day brings, His help is assured.

So today, dear mama, run to your Refuge and cling to His embrace. In the midst of your jumbled thoughts, His comforting presence will speak peace to your soul. Be reminded that you are never truly alone, for Jesus has ensured your eternal connection through His sacrifice on the cross. The resurrection stands as a powerful reminder that even in your darkest moments, God's love prevails. He is indeed our refuge and strength, an ever-present help in trouble.

God,

You are my Refuge and my Strength,
the One who will never leave,
whose love will always prevail.
I run to You and find rest and peace.

Amen.

THE JOURNEY OF FORGIVENESS

Then Peter came to him and asked,
"Lord, how often should I forgive someone
who sins against me? Seven times?"
"No, not seven times," Jesus replied,
"but seventy times seven!"

MATTHEW 18:21–22

Some of the wounds we receive from others are mere inconveniences, like stumbling over a stone in our path. We brush ourselves off and carry on, hardly giving it a second thought. They say not to sweat the small stuff, and for good reason. But at the other end of the spectrum are wounds that cut deep, leaving us gasping for air and struggling to form coherent thoughts. The pain is both intense and numbing, lingering for years and causing our knees to wobble at the mere thought.

In the midst of my marital separation, forgiveness became a daunting challenge. How do you forgive the unforgivable? At times, I found myself wrestling with the very idea of extending forgiveness. But true forgiveness isn't about conjuring up immense feelings of goodwill toward those who've wronged us; it's about positioning ourselves at the cross, where we become both recipients and conduits of God's boundless grace.

This journey of forgiveness is a humbling process, one where we continually circle back to the foot of the cross, allowing the living Christ within us to guide our actions. It's about emptying ourselves before Him, allowing His grace to fill us and empower us to extend forgiveness—even to those who've hurt us the most.

As we walk this path of forgiveness, we not only experience healing ourselves, but we become models for our children as they navigate their own journeys of forgiveness. Through the Spirit's work within us, we can display a grace that transcends human understanding, demonstrating what it means to live out forgiveness in our everyday lives.

Begin to embrace this journey of forgiveness, as much as you can, dear mama, knowing that as you humble yourself before the Lord, He is faithful to fill you with His grace and empower you to extend forgiveness to others, no matter how deep the wounds may be.

Lord,

I choose to forgive. Help me to walk it out, letting go of the hurt and the pain and moving forward in Your light and love.

Amen.

HAPPILY EVER AFTER

The Lord is close
to the brokenhearted and saves those
who are crushed in spirit.
PSALM 34:18 NIV

In the stories we cherished as children, hope always triumphs, leading to the famous line, "And they all lived happily ever after." But in the real world, tales often take on a more somber tone, resembling tragedies where life shatters, leaving someone to pick up the broken pieces. So, what then?

When my own world crumbled, I found myself curled up, thinking, "I'll never be okay again." It felt like an abyss of devastation I was unprepared for. Or was I? Looking back, I realized my past struggles—infertility, miscarriages, depression, and marital woes—had taught me something invaluable: amid the ruins, God's goodness, faithfulness, and unwavering love remained steadfast. In that moment, that foundation mattered more than ever. Our circumstances might have changed irreversibly, but God remained unchanged.

God's promise to draw near to the brokenhearted isn't just a comforting sentiment; it's a reality that was demonstrated when Jesus Himself entered our fallen, sin-sickened world and bore our brokenness on the cross. When life shatters, and we're left holding the fragments, we face a choice: either try to piece things back together alone or entrust our brokenness to our Redeemer at the foot of the cross. When we choose the latter, He tenderly gathers the shards in His nail-scarred hands, promising to weave them into something beautiful beyond our imagination. Our God, who wields the power of resurrection, is always faithful to turn our tragedies into triumphs.

Lord,

my happily-ever-after isn't what I expected it to be,
but I know You have an even better ending to my story
prepared in Your grand and glorious plan.
I trust You to finish what You've started in my life,
and I'm excited to see what comes
next in my journey with You!

Amen.

HE'S READY TO LISTEN

Hear my cry for help,
my King and my God, for to You I pray.

PSALM 5:2 NIV

Prayer isn't just a ritual; it's an ongoing conversation, a lifeline connecting us to God's unfailing love and wisdom. I've found myself in a perpetual dialogue with Him, where "amen" isn't the end, but rather a continuous exchange of thanksgiving, questions, pleas for change—and even requests for mundane things like finding lost car keys. The beauty of it all is that God embraces every aspect of our communication, from our deepest doubts to our smallest concerns.

Yet, there are moments when life feels heavy, and our prayers seem to echo into silence. I've been there, too, wrestling with the frustration of feeling unheard. But in those moments, I've learned to lean into trust, knowing that even when it seems like God is silent, He's always at work behind the scenes, orchestrating events in ways we couldn't imagine. He not only hears our prayers but also aligns them with His perfect plan, weaving every circumstance together for our ultimate good.

As a single mother, I've encountered countless

situations where I've desperately needed God's intervention. But I've also experienced the profound peace that comes from centering my life around His guidance. When I intentionally sought His voice amid the chaos, I discovered a wellspring of wisdom and direction that carried me through even the darkest of days. And it's in those moments of trust that I've witnessed the miraculous unfold, leading me to a place of restoration beyond my wildest dreams.

If today you find yourself in the midst of uncertainty or despair, remember that you're never alone in your journey. God is always there, ready to listen, guide, and lead you into a life filled with His unending grace and provision. Trust in His faithfulness, and you'll soon look back on your path with a heart overflowing with gratitude, knowing without a doubt that He has been with you every step of the way.

Lord,

thank You for Your listening ear.
I bring to You all my worries
and burdens and lay them at Your feet.
I will listen for Your voice and
then do what You say to do.

Amen.

THINK ON THESE THINGS

Finally, brothers and sisters,
whatever is true, whatever is noble,
whatever is right, whatever is pure,
whatever is lovely, whatever is admirable—
if anything is excellent or praiseworthy—
think about such things.

PHILIPPIANS 4:8 NIV

Negativity can sneak into our minds like a stealthy intruder, filling our thoughts with anger, jealousy, and self-doubt. It's all too common to dwell on the things that go wrong or the disagreements with our co-parent, allowing bitterness to take root and overshadow the positives in our lives. But dwelling in negativity only leads to a dark and heavy burden.

Instead of allowing negativity to consume us, we have the power to shift our focus. Rather than fixating on what's wrong, we can choose to embrace what is true, noble, right, pure, lovely, admirable, excellent, and praiseworthy. Even amid life's challenges, there is still goodness to be found—God's love surrounds us, and our efforts as mothers are bringing wonderful blessings into our children's lives.

Today, let's make a conscious effort to redirect our

thoughts. Instead of dwelling on negativity, let's pause and acknowledge the blessings in our lives. Take a moment to appreciate the love and support that surrounds you and recognize the strength and resilience within yourself. By shifting our focus to the goodness that abounds, we can lighten the weight of negativity and find renewed peace and joy in God's abundant grace.

Take a break from the cycle of negative thinking. Give yourself permission to rest in the goodness of God and the beauty of your own efforts as a mother. Embrace the truth of your blessings, and let gratitude fill your heart. As we choose to focus on the positive, we invite God's light to shine brightly within us, illuminating the path forward with hope and joy.

Father,

I choose to monitor my thoughts today.
When negativity tries to creep in, teach me
how to redirect my thoughts in a positive direction.
Reading and meditating on Your Word
is a great place to start!
Shine Your light in me and through me this day.

Amen.

A BEAUTIFUL WORK OF HIS HAND

Yet You, Lord, are our Father.
We are the clay, You are the potter;
we are all the work of Your hand.
ISAIAH 64:8 NIV

In the Bible, God is often depicted as a potter, and we are likened to clay. This analogy beautifully illustrates our relationship with God. A potter skillfully molds earthenware from clay, a process that involves spinning and intense heat.

Sometimes, in the shaping process, the pottery may crack or break. Yet, even broken pieces can be repurposed to create something stronger. Potters grind these broken fragments down and then mix them with soft clay to reinforce it. The resulting mixture retains its flexibility—while gaining strength from the broken particles. With the right balance, the potter molds the clay on the wheel, shaping it into exquisite bowls, jars, and other creations.

When our hopes are dashed or our dreams seem shattered, it's comforting to know that God specializes in redeeming brokenness. He takes the shattered pieces of our lives, infuses them with the fresh hope of His love, and helps us reshape our dreams. Like clay that is strengthened by previously broken pieces, we can allow God to take the broken remnants of our past and make us stronger as we move forward with Him.

If you're feeling broken or discouraged today, remember that God is the ultimate Potter. He has the remarkable ability to transform your brokenness into something beautiful and purposeful. Trust in His redemption process and allow Him to work in your life. As you surrender your brokenness to Him, He will mold you into a masterpiece, stronger and more resilient than ever before.

Dear Potter,

You are so kind as You lovingly shape my heart and my life. Thank You for making something beautiful out of my mess. I'm willing to be molded and used by You. Love always, Your Moldable Clay.

Amen.

RESTORATION AWAITS

In all your ways know and acknowledge and recognize Him, and He will make your paths straight and smooth [removing obstacles that block your way].

PROVERBS 3:6 AMP

Navigating life after divorce can feel like an uphill battle, even when you're committed to surrendering everything to God and embracing new beginnings. Despite your best efforts to move forward, the past has a sneaky way of lingering. Whether it's reminders that come from family members, communication with your ex-partner about shared responsibilities, or lingering financial burdens, it can feel like your past mistakes are constantly haunting you. But take heart—you *can* overcome.

The challenges of the past can resurface whether the other parent is actively involved or not. Personally, I thought my divorce would bring closure, but instead, it marked the beginning of a long and arduous journey. From ongoing custody disputes to financial struggles, it seemed like the road ahead was endless.

Do you ever feel like reminders of your past mistakes are haunting you like ghosts from a Charles Dickens novel? They can lead you down memory lane to moments you'd rather forget. Yet, amid it all, I remind myself that God has never failed me. Every battle I've faced, I've emerged from stronger. Knowing that I've overcome every challenge so far gives me confidence that I'll overcome whatever I'm facing now.

Perhaps as you read this, you're wondering how you'll muster the strength for another day of challenges. But if you keep your gaze fixed on the One who never lets you down, you'll find the courage to rise above the circumstances that are trying to drag you down. It won't necessarily get easier overnight—often, it doesn't—but your unwavering faith that you will overcome and that restoration awaits in your story will be your guiding light through the uncertainty.

Allow the Spirit of God, who resides within your heart and mind, to propel you forward and lift you above the arms of your past that seek to pull you back. With His strength, you can face each day with resilience, knowing that you are not defined by your past but by the hope and promise of your future.

Lord,

I long for Your restoration power to work in my life. I fix my gaze upon You as I choose to look forward and face each new day with You.

Amen.

BE AN EXAMPLE

Don't copy the behavior and customs of this world,
but let God transform you into a new person
by changing the way you think.
Then you will learn to know God's will for you,
which is good and pleasing and perfect.

ROMANS 12:2

I don't know what the spiritual rituals and routines are at your house. I know that at mine, it's hard to find a time for family devotions when everyone is at home and able to be together at the same time on a consistent basis. And yet, we do—I have read individual devotions with my kids at bedtime, or together as a family at dinnertime—whatever works for us in the stage of life we are in is what we do!

As single parents, we shoulder the responsibility of being the spiritual leaders in our households. To hear from the Lord and then provide spiritual wisdom to our children takes a measure of discipline in our own lives. We may have to be intentional about carving out those moments because life has a way of becoming overwhelmingly noisy. Some days, finding moments of quiet and solace feels like an impossible task amid the chaos, doesn't it?

Investing time in reading the Word, praying, and

meditating not only makes us more attuned to God's voice but it also leaves a noticeable void when we neglect these practices. Consider setting aside time for you and God after the kids are in bed, when you cultivate a habit of focusing on the Lord through prayer and reading—not just books about His Word, but the Bible itself, which is where we find our life. Or, if you find it hard to focus some nights, simply listen to worship music and pray. Allow yourself to unwind and bask in God's presence. Worship can serve as a refreshing escape, especially during the toughest moments of the day when your mind is racing.

Invite God into your daily routine. The rewards of spending time in His presence are abundant. You'll experience peace, wisdom, guidance, freedom, love, and fulfillment. And by prioritizing these moments of spiritual nourishment, you'll notice a profound impact on the atmosphere of your home. This is truly the greatest gift you can give yourself and your family—the gift of a household filled with the presence and peace of God.

Lord,

You have chosen me to be the mother of these precious children. Help me teach them and guide them into a wonderful, long-lasting relationship with You.

Amen.

THE LORD GIVES STRENGTH TO HIS PEOPLE.

Psalm 29:11 NIV

TUNE IN TO THE KIDS

Train up a child in the way he should go;
even when he is old he will not depart from it.

PROVERBS 22:6 ESV

Life has a way of turning our focus inward, especially during challenging times. In the circumstances that brought you into single motherhood, your children may have been too young to grasp the situation or old enough to ask questions—either situation can be challenging. My own divorce journey was marked by betrayal, heartache, and abuse, and at the time, it was difficult to see beyond my own pain, despite knowing my children were hurting too.

If your story includes a messy divorce or a failed relationship, you've likely experienced deep wounds that need time to heal. It's crucial to allow yourself space for grief and growth. Yet, even as you travel your own journey, it's important to also tune in to your children's needs and emotions.

Our children are deeply connected to our hearts. They absorb our emotions and process them right alongside us. When they can't fully comprehend what's happening, it can lead to confusion and added distress. And if they've witnessed the separation of their parents—especially if there was a great deal of conflict involved—their pain can often mirror our own.

As mothers, we have the power to navigate life transitions in a way that minimizes the impact on our children. While they may not need all the details, they will still benefit greatly from open and honest communication. Empathy is key; by understanding and sharing their feelings, we create a safe and loving environment for them to navigate life's challenges.

Today, dear mama, ask the Lord for the wisdom you need to connect with your children on a deeper level, to empathize with their emotions, and to provide a listening ear during difficult times. Remember, your presence and love are guiding them not only through life's trials but also toward the unwavering love of their heavenly Father, who will never abandon them.

Lord,

help me tune in to the needs of my children—
spoken and unspoken. Help me to listen to their
heart cries and give them what they need.

Amen.

GUARD YOUR HEART!

Guard your heart above all else,
for it determines the course of your life.

PROVERBS 4:23

What if the fears and worries consuming your thoughts never materialize? Picture a future where you and your ex are on good terms, your children are thriving, and life is filled with happiness. Consider the possibility that all the energy spent on worry could be better invested in moments shared with your children.

As mothers, it's natural for worry and fear to try to find their way into our minds. However, we must stand strong against them. Dwelling on "what-if" scenarios not only drains our energy but also steals precious moments of rest. Instead of finding peace at the end of a long day, we find ourselves tangled in anxious thoughts.

Changing our thought patterns is a process that takes time and effort. We must recognize when negative thoughts creep in and gradually shift our focus. When worries about our children's safety or well-being arise, we're actually causing unnecessary stress on our bodies. We're reacting to hypothetical situations that haven't occurred, triggering stress responses that harm us.

But what if we shifted our perspective? What if we trusted that God is guiding our steps and orchestrating our lives for good? What if every challenge we face strengthens us and leads to a brighter future? Even when fear tries to grip our minds, we can choose to focus on the truth and allow it to guide our thoughts.

Lord,

I hand my what-ifs over to You today,
choosing to guard my heart.
I trust You. Thank You for
working all things together for my good.

Amen.

A BRIGHT FUTURE

***"So don't worry about tomorrow,
for tomorrow will bring its own worries.
Today's trouble is enough for today."***

MATTHEW 6:34

God's knowledge encompasses every aspect of our lives, from the length of our days to the paths our children will tread, from their triumphs to their stumbles. Every moment, every achievement, and every setback is woven together by His loving hands for His divine purpose. Yet, despite this assurance, the unknown future can still provoke fear within us.

As human beings, uncertainty about tomorrow is inherent to our existence. We cannot predict the twists and turns of life, whether it's the duration of our earthly journey, the outcome of a loved one's battle with illness, or the choices our children will make. The future remains a realm of mystery, where even the most careful plans can be overturned by unforeseen circumstances.

Yet, amid this uncertainty, there is solace in knowing that while we may not hold the answers to what lies ahead, our heavenly Father does. He who tenderly consoles us in our moments of fear and sorrow is intimately acquainted with every detail of our future. Take comfort in the knowledge that the One who holds the universe in His hands also holds you and your children close to His heart.

Father,

despite the uncertainty in my life right now,
I know my future is in Your capable hands.
I choose to trust in You and not worry.
You have good things planned for me.

Amen.

A NEW PERSPECTIVE

The faithful love of the Lord never ends!
His mercies never cease.
Great is His faithfulness;
His mercies begin afresh each morning.
LAMENTATIONS 3:22–23

When the shadows of hopelessness start to loom, it's a signal for revival to take place within you. As you rise above challenges, your spirit gains strength, and you realize that difficulties don't have the final say. The Bible often refers to these trials as "afflictions," signifying the depth of pain and suffering they can bring. Illness, heartache, disaster, loss, and failure are just a few examples of what can lead to this sense of hopelessness.

But in the face of adversity, refuse to succumb to despair. Instead, turn to the book of Lamentations, where you'll find the spark of revival you need. It reminds us that God's love never wavers, even in our darkest moments. Each morning, His love and compassion are renewed, offering a beacon of hope amid the despair.

Sometimes all it takes is a moment of pause and reflection to discover a new perspective on our problems. With every small victory and the unwavering love of God guiding us, hope begins to stir once more, and our burdens feel a little lighter. So, let a smile brighten your face and let joy fill your heart as you breathe new life into your hopes and dreams, knowing that God's love is always there to revive and restore.

Lord,

I choose to place my hope in You.
Thank You for giving me a new perspective
on what I am facing today.
With You by my side,
I know things will always turn out
for my good in the end.

Amen.

LOVE YOUR ENEMIES

"Love your enemies! Do good to them.
Lend to them without expecting to be repaid.
Then your reward from heaven will be very great,
and you will truly be acting as children of the Most High,
for He is kind to those who are unthankful and wicked."

LUKE 6:35

Among the many commandments in the Bible, few are as challenging as "Love your enemies." It's not just about tolerating them or doing them favors to show off our moral superiority; Jesus calls us to genuinely love them. Yes, even those who have treated us with hate, cruelty, or dishonesty. Whether it's the church member spreading rumors, the friend who betrayed us, the boss who seems relentless, or even our ex-partner.

Loving our enemies can feel like an uphill battle, especially when resentment and hurt linger in our hearts. That's why prayer is essential. We need to continually seek God's strength, grace, and patience to extend love to those who have wronged us. And as we pray, we can also ask for the willingness to forgive and the humility to seek reconciliation.

Moreover, in our prayers, we might discover our own

struggles with bitterness. As we intercede for our enemies and strive to mend broken relationships, we may realize that they are just as beloved by God as we are. Despite their flaws and faults, God's love extends to them, too, prompting us to extend forgiveness and grace, just as we have received from our heavenly Father.

Lord,

sometimes Your commands aren't easy to follow, but with Your help, I choose to forgive those who have hurt me. Whether or not reconciliation is possible in this lifetime, I seek Your peace in these challenging relationships—and in my own heart. Thank You for Your goodness and grace.

Amen.

SOMEONE WHO UNDERSTANDS

This High Priest of ours
understands our weaknesses,
for He faced all of the same testings we do,
yet He did not sin. So let us come boldly
to the throne of our gracious God.
There we will receive His mercy,
and we will find grace to help us
when we need it most.

HEBREWS 4:15–16

Life as a single parent can easily overwhelm us. Yet, God is so happy to reveal His strength in our weakness. In our darkest moments, He shines His light, turning our struggles into stories of triumph. Our pain becomes a testimony, ministering to others and making us more compassionate souls. Indeed, God brings beauty from ashes.

In times of distress, it's comforting to know that Jesus understands our suffering intimately. He experienced rejection, abandonment, and agony firsthand. And despite His trials, He exemplified the security found in aligning with God's will.

Jesus often withdrew to spend quiet moments with

the Father, finding solace and strength in His presence. In these intimate encounters, He received nourishment for His soul and the fortitude to endure. Following His example, we, too, can find peace and renewal by seeking God in stillness.

When we carve out time to connect with our heavenly Father, we undergo transformation. He welcomes us with open arms, offering us peace and strength. And although He delights in our love and praise, it is His love that sustains us, not the other way around.

As we bask in God's love, we find security and renewal. Approaching Him with gratitude and praise, our hearts and minds are refreshed. His love envelops us, drawing us closer to Him with each moment spent in His presence, just as Jesus experienced when He spent time with the Father.

Lord,

spending time with You is so refreshing.
You understand what I'm going through—You get it!
When I pour out my heart to You, You comfort me and
give me guidance and strength to carry on. I am so
thankful for Your understanding and Your love!

Amen.

TRUE LOVE

"For the mountains may move
and the hills disappear,
but even then My faithful love
for you will remain."
ISAIAH 54:10

Love is a concept that saturates our culture, appearing in countless songs, movies, and TV shows. However, much of what we encounter in modern media falls short of true love. Pop singers often sing of a shallow infatuation, driven by selfish desires or fleeting emotions.

God, the ultimate Author of love, designed it to be so much more. Love isn't merely a feeling; it's a deliberate choice, a commitment that endures through thick and thin. It's a marathon, requiring dedication and ongoing effort, even when reciprocation is lacking.

The love Jesus demonstrated through His sacrifice exemplifies this selfless commitment. Despite knowing that many would reject His love, He chose to give Himself for us. Similarly, God's love for us is unwavering, transcending our mistakes and doubts. He loves us unconditionally, offering forgiveness, acceptance, and perfect love.

Despite the superficial portrayals of love in media, we

are reminded of the genuine love we receive from God. This love serves as a model for how we should love others and what we should seek in our own relationships. Let's strive to emulate God's love, extending it to those around us and seeking it in our interactions with others.

Lord,

although the love of other human beings tends to be fickle and shallow, there one day and gone another, Your love is steadfast and sure. Teach me how to love others the way that You love them—and me! Remind me, in the midst of a culture that glorifies human love, that Your love supersedes them all. Thank You for loving me!

Amen.

WHAT'S YOUR WORTH?

But you are the ones chosen by God,
chosen for the high calling of priestly work,
chosen to be a holy people, God's instruments
to do His work and speak out for Him,
to tell others of the night-and-day difference
He made for you—from nothing to something,
from rejected to accepted.

I PETER 2:9–10 THE MESSAGE

Imagine someone asking you, "Who are you?" How would you respond?

Many of us might define ourselves by our job titles, financial status, or social media presence. We often measure our worth by external factors, seeking validation in the world's eyes. Yet none of these things truly encapsulate our essence. In fact, they can lead to a perpetual sense of discontentment, as we chase after fleeting achievements and elusive standards of perfection.

But what if we took a different approach? What if we chose to embrace ourselves as God made us—flaws and all? To recognize that despite our imperfections, we are inherently good, kindhearted, and valuable individuals. As single mothers, we are hardworking, resilient, and fiercely devoted to our families.

Accepting ourselves doesn't mean settling for mediocrity or refusing to grow. Instead, it's about recognizing our intrinsic worth and allowing that realization to fuel our personal growth journey.

Lord Jesus,

no matter what role I need to take on today—
mother, sister, friend, cab driver, housecleaner, cook—
You are with me, and You accept me just as I am.
I know You love me despite my flaws; I choose to
love myself, as well, and move forward into the
wonderful future You have prepared for me.

Amen.

TAKE CARE OF YOURSELF!

Cast your cares on the LORD
and He will sustain you;
He will never let the righteous
be shaken.

PSALM 55:22 NIV

In today's world, the spectrum of single motherhood is vast and varied. Some of us have been widowed at a young age. Some of us have had children without getting married, or even decide to adopt while still remaining single. Others find themselves in a semi-single state while their partners serve in the military, deployed for extended periods of time.

Then there are those, like me, who are single moms due to divorce.

Despite our diverse circumstances, we share a common struggle: How do we prioritize self-care while also caring for our families? Every single mom I know wrestles with this concept. We're natural caregivers, constantly focused on the well-being of our children. But what about our own needs?

It's crucial to recognize that we need care too. We can't pour from an empty cup. When we engage in self-care practices, we're not indulging ourselves; we're acknowledging our humanity and the necessity to replenish ourselves physically, mentally, and spiritually.

Dear single mama, know this: God welcomes our vulnerability and our admission of weakness. He delights in our honesty when we come to Him with our needs, including the need to care for ourselves. In surrendering to Him, we honor His love and provision for us.

In the middle of a culture that glorifies hustle and achievement, Jesus offers us a different path—a path of rest and restoration. He invites us to lay down our burdens and find solace in His love. Self-care, then, becomes an act of obedience—a response to His tender invitation to care for ourselves as He cares for us.

Let's heed His gentle call to slow down, to nurture our bodies, minds, and souls. As we care for ourselves, we honor the temple He has entrusted to us, demonstrating our gratitude for His boundless love and grace.

Lord,

help me to slow down today,

take care of myself, and spend time with You.

Thank You for Your love!

Amen.

WRITING YOUR STORY

See what great love
the Father has lavished on us,
that we should be called children of God!
And that is what we are!

1 JOHN 3:1 NIV

You are a genuine miracle. God has called you to tasks beyond your wildest imagination. No matter what you have been through in the past, the incredible thing about Jesus is His knack for rewriting our stories. By surrendering to Him and His guidance, you can live out the most extraordinary, exhilarating, unexpected life with Him by your side.

What's truly remarkable about your journey is that it's an opportunity for God to astound you. I'm talking about the kind of miracles that make you want to dance around the room and shout with joy. Who knows what good things are coming your way that will fill you with more happiness than you ever thought possible?

Do we really want to navigate life on our own terms? For a long time, the path I was on felt like I was stumbling through one of those carnival mazes—with the crazy mirrors and no way out. But when I relinquished control to God, surrendered my desires, and trusted that His plans were far greater than mine, things started falling into place.

Your life, dear mama, is a complete miracle. Your existence itself is a testament to God's grace and power. Trust wholeheartedly that God can take any worry or shame you carry and transform it into a beautiful testimony of His grace and love. And He has dreams, opportunities, and blessings in store for you that will leave everyone around you in awe of the wonderful and awesome God you serve.

Father,

thank You for making me a miracle,
and for doing wondrous miracles in my life.
I will tell others about Your love today and
the amazing things You have done for me!

Amen.

THIS IS WHAT
THE LORD SAYS:
“STAND AT THE
CROSSROADS
AND LOOK;
ASK FOR
THE ANCIENT
PATHS,